Mémé Santerre

Mémé Santerre
A French Woman of the People

SERGE GRAFTEAUX

Translated by Louise A. Tilly
and Kathryn L. Tilly

Edited with an Introduction
by Louise A. Tilly

SCHOCKEN BOOKS • NEW YORK

First published by Schocken Books 1985

10 9 8 7 6 5 4 3 2 1   85 86 87 88

Library of Congress Cataloging in Publication Data
Santerre, Mémé, 1891–1977
Mémé Santerre : a French woman of the people.
Memoirs of Mémé Santerre as told to Serge Grafteaux.
Translation of: Mémé Santerre.
Bibliography: p.
1. Santerre, Mémé, 1891–1977. 2. Avesnes (Nord, France)—Biography.
3. Avesnes (Nord, France)—Social life and customs.
I. Grafteaux, Serge. II. Tilly, Louise. III. Title.
DC801.A95S26713   1985   944'.28 [B]   85–2038

Design by Ann Gold
Manufactured in the United States of America
ISBN 0–8052–3954–5

Contents

Introduction to the English-language Edition   *vii*

Mémé Santerre   *1*

Chronology   *167*

Notes   *169*

Introduction
to the English-language Edition

This is the life story of Marie-Catherine Gardez, later the wife of Auguste Santerre. In her old age, when she told her story to Serge Grafteaux, a French journalist, she was known as Mémé, the familiar term for Grandmother. Born in northern France, not far from the Belgian border, Mémé was a simple woman who worked most of her life at humble callings: hand weaving, farm labor, domestic service. A native of the most industrialized region of France, she nevertheless lived apart from industrial work and large cities. A citizen of a highly centralized parliamentary nation-state, she had little formal knowledge of French government and national or international politics. Yet, processes and events far beyond her control affected her life in deep and far-reaching ways. The industrial capitalist economy and the nation-state are the essential context of her life. It is the purpose of this introduction to supply this large context into which her deeply personal but historically significant memories fit.

The Economy of France and the Nord
at the End of the Nineteenth Century

The dominant theme of the first chapters of *Mémé Santerre* is the regime of work in which she and her natal family were enmeshed. The relationship of the curious backwater of hand production of textiles with the French industrial economy is central here. The eighteenth-century Industrial Revolution in England had initiated a massive shift of labor and resources away from primary production—agriculture, fishing, forestry—toward manufacturing, commerce, and service activities. The scale of production grew, and the factory eventually replaced the household as the most common unit of production. In France, industrialization came later, and its pace was more gradual; it affected different categories of workers and geographic areas at different rates and times. At the same time, in striking contrast to England, peasant agriculture persisted in France. There was even a tendency through the nineteenth century that saw increasing numbers of small peasants, and little decrease in the proportion of peasants, in the population. In most parts of France, agricultural production was done primarily by peasants who worked within household units on land that they owned or controlled. However, Mémé and her family were not part of the peasant economy. They were rural proletarians.

Proletarianization is the process by which the proportion of people whose survival depended on the sale of their labor increased. It went along with the growth of scale in manufacturing and agriculture. The distinguishing feature of proletarians is their wage earning. Proletarians were dependent on others to provide wage work and produce their food for them; they had lost the small measure of control that peasants or craftworkers had in these areas. For many ordinary people experiencing the growth of industrial capitalism, proletarianization was the central social experience.

The process occurred in rural and urban settings. As the scale of production increased, there was a decline of small units of production and fewer skilled craft producers who controlled the tempo and quality of their own work. More and more people became wage workers in capitalist-owned industry. In rural areas, members of peasant households whose labor was not needed left to find wage labor elsewhere. If holdings were subdivided to provide an inheritance for several children, they could become too small to support a family. Capitalist farmers could purchase these to build large holdings, which they would run with wage labor. This offered wages for those without land adequate to support themselves and their families. Supplemental wage labor could also be had in manufacturing—often hand weaving—which was done in rural or village households.

This kind of transitional or protoindustrial production was not subsistence manufacture for home use. It produced for a market, and was typically controlled by capitalists with an urban base. Domestic industry, as it has been called, had begun much earlier in various regions near big cities, as a stratagem of merchant capitalists to tap underemployed—hence inexpensive— labor power in needy rural households. It lingered in France even in the late nineteenth century, because it guaranteed reliable craftsmanship and provided the possibility of quick changeover of styles to match fashions, not to mention low wages and capital costs for the capitalists. By the period of which Mémé writes, many families in the villages of the Cambrai region where hand weaving was concentrated owned only their tools, not land. Despite this ownership of a small amount of capital—in this case, their looms—they were proletarians, parents and children alike selling their labor power with little control over the conditions of their work.

French Politics and the French State

Although France had long been a centralized state, the French Revolution of 1789–95 ended the old monarchy, and with it the politics of privilege and the corporate rights of guilds, communities, and region. A parliamentary regime based on a constitution was established. The revolutionary and imperial periods saw a series of political systems. In the nineteenth century, there was continued debate and political struggle over who was to be permitted to participate in politics, and under what conditions. A restored and then a constitutional monarchy were followed by a revolution in 1848 which established a new republic. Universal manhood suffrage was passed. This Second Republic was short-lived, to be replaced in its turn by a new empire, with Louis Napoleon as emperor. The Second Empire fell in 1870, destroyed by the war with Prussia that its rulers had welcomed. Political ideology still divided Frenchmen rather than uniting them, but a new republic, the third, emerged in the 1870s as a compromise to restore orderly rule. The Third Republic was the state under which Mémé Santerre grew up and lived most of her life.

The constitutional laws of the Third Republic continued universal male suffrage and parliamentary government. Most of the ministries that held office from the late nineteenth century to the 1930s were conservative on economic and social issues. Laws enabling workers to organize and establishing the right to strike were passed, but frequent government intervention in strikes and worker politics occurred. There was very little social legislation, beyond the laws establishing universal compulsory free schooling, complete by 1886. The lay schools were seen as instruments of the state in forming citizens.[1] Male schoolteachers in small towns served frequently as secretary of the town hall, a kind of fringe benefit for the poorly paid teacher and a link committing him to the state system. Mayors, although elected locally, were representatives of the French nation and attempted to administer centrally generated laws and regulations in uniform ways throughout the country. Teachers in the state schools were also employees of the centralized state and representatives of the nation; they taught a centrally established curriculum from standard texts to students preparing to pass national examinations.

Opposition to this extremely centralized, bureaucratic state came from various groups. Some were regional, although these were less important than in earlier or later periods. Others were based on social class and religion. The aristocracy continued to long for a return to monarchic or imperial government. It was allied most often with other faithful supporters of the Roman Catholic church; bitter political struggles were waged along the lines of church–state relations. Catholic grievances went back to the period of the Great Revolution, when church property had been confiscated and sold for the benefit of the state. Strict government control over the church and its members was instituted. A compromise was worked out in a concordat between pope and emperor in 1801. Catholicism was declared to be the religion of the majority of the French, and the clergy became state employees. During periods of monarchical and imperial regimes in the nineteenth century, the clerical role in education was permitted to increase. In many parts of France, by the 1870's, schools that were public in the sense that they were owned and financed by communities and state were staffed by male and female members of religious orders. The inhabitants of all classes of the department of the Nord, where Mémé was born and spent her youth, were renowned for their practicing Catholicism and their faithfulness to the church. Only in the late nineteenth century did secularism develop in urban industrial areas of the department among workers, and to some extent in the middle class.

The central governments of the Third Republic, however, were dominated by politicians committed to a secular ideal of the state. The field of the struggle between practicing Catholics and the state was the schools. There were two drives to secularize the schools. The first concentrated on eliminating religious teachers, but also tried to remove symbols of the church, such as crucifixes, from the classrooms. This first drive to laicize the schools, orchestrated by Jules Ferry, took place from 1879 to 1882; its goal was "to break the hold of Catholicism over future generations and to unite the supporters of the Republic."[2] This effort was gradualist: religious teachers would be replaced on a phased plan. Its results were incomplete, partly because there were not enough lay teachers, partly because of foot-dragging or more vigorous opposition from Catholics in some areas. The second drive was part of a much more far-reaching political effort: a law in 1904 decreed the separation of church and state and the confiscation of church property. Lay associations were to govern parishes and administer the churches. The concordat was abrogated unilaterally by the French government, without consultation with the church hierarchy or its faithful. There was little flexibility in this extreme law. This time noisy objections were accompanied by violence when government officials attempted to inventory church property, including the precious metal ojects in the holy tabernacle of each church, as required by law. Accommodations were worked out over the years before World War I. The war, with its drawing together of the nation under attack and the suspension of political disagreements (and occasional suppression of dissent), marked the end of bitter anticlericalism and equally bitter Catholic intransigence.

The other major group opposing the Third Republic was the socialists, in France a fragmented group, not a single party. Socialists generally supported radical changes in the organization of production, including the expropriation of capital, and they usually took part in electoral politics. They refused, however, to become members of governments and generally eschewed alliances of any formal sort. Socialists supported republicans on the issue of lay schools, but they separated from most of the conservative governments on economic and social issues. Although committed to the Second Socialist International principles of worker solidarity across national boundaries, the socialists of France, like most European socialists, supported their nation's entry into World War I. Those who dissented were branded traitors, and their speech and action repressed. The war, therefore, marked a break in socialist opposition to the state, as it did of Catholic. Most of the interwar period of the 1920s and 1930s was marked by low-key or no opposition on the part of workers and socialists. The rebuilding of leftist opposition will be discussed after an examination of the consequences of World War I for France and the Nord.

France, the Nord, and World War I

Although France is counted one of the victors of the war of 1914–1918, it suffered staggering losses. Its total wounded and dead, 5.5 million, was smaller than the German 6 million, but it constituted a larger proportion of the smaller French population. Huge battles like that of Verdun produced casualties of 300,000 on the French and German sides. Since most of the fighting in the west took place on French soil, civilian casualties were significant and property damage enormous. Homes, factories, monuments were destroyed. Farm animals were lost. Mines were flooded. As France suffered disproportionately among the western combatants, so too the Nord suffered disproportionately in France.

It is still dotted with military cemeteries from the period. The death registers of each town and village bear testimony to the war's impact on civilian mortality. The Monument aux Morts that stands in the square in front of the church of Avesnes-les-Aubert tells the story: 1,600 were lost, and civilian casualties outnumbered military ones by ten to one. Some 36 percent of the inhabitants died in the war.

The losses of the war contributed to the French desire to punish Germany economically, which would thus allow France to recover some of her lost resources. Rebuilding was slow, however, because of population losses and the enormity of the damage. Economic growth was interrupted and concentration slowed. Employer resistance to worker demands stiffened. The nation entered a conservative political phase during which international concerns were foremost.

The Depression, Nazism, and the Coming of World War II

The forward motion of rebuilding the economy and agricultural prosperity relative to the rest of Europe brought France to the Depression in an economically strong position. Nevertheless, the Depression's effect was eventually felt, as exports and then production declined. The coming to power of the Nazis in Germany was paralleled by a growth of extremist right-wing political groups in France, offering conservative economic solutions to her problems and venomous antisocialist propaganda. The German militarization of the Rhineland, forbidden by the peace treaties ending World War I, occurred without decisive opposition by France. Worker dissatisfaction with government inaction on domestic economic problems and socialist and radical belief that a stronger stand was needed against the Nazis brought them into a coalition with the Communists in the 1936 elections. The Popular Front election, as it was called, was unusual in the clearly stated right and left positions on internal and international issues. The Popular Front won a decisive victory and a coalition government was installed, with the Socialists entering the government as a party.

Léon Blum, the Socialist prime minister, set social reform as the government's first priority. A wave of sit-down strikes supported his policy, and the government forced employers to make important concessions to their workers, including paid holidays. These concessions simply brought French labor relations closer to those already prevailing in most western countries. The armaments industry was nationalized, and government control over banks increased. These actions exacerbated domestic political differences and alarmed conservative French business and financial leaders. There was a large-scale flight of investment capital out of France, forcing devaluation of the franc. Blum was obliged to halt his reform efforts, and within two years a series of modifications in the composition of the government had restored it to the old, familiar conservative cast.

Opposition to the social and economic programs of the Popular Front government was often joined to disapproval of its strong antifascist stand. Divisions among French voters and politicans, then, contributed to a weak position in face of the Nazis and inadequate military preparation in response to German aggressive policy and behavior. Since the last war had been a war of defense, a defensive strategy was pursued: the heavily fortified Maginot Line on France's eastern border was believed to be adequate to stop any German advance.

World War II started in September 1939, with the German invasion of Poland. It was more than six months, however, before the Nazis struck France, again advancing through Belgium. This time, however, their lightning attack, the blitzkrieg, overwhelmed France with dazzling speed. France's military defense collapsed, and its civilian populations fled the war zones. The fall of France came within five weeks; most of France was then occupied by a German military force.

Coerced and/or collaborating, the French produced agricultural and industrial products for the German war effort. Resistance gradually coalesced, however, and a formal organization representing various political parties and Catholic associations was established. The Nazis severely repressed resistance efforts, sometimes by random punishment of persons in the town or area where an attack on Germans or their collaborators had occurred. The war years were hard, with food and fuel shortages and anxiety piled on top of great physical danger for anyone who protested or, even more, took action to resist. Although France suffered a good deal of damage and heavy human losses from the fighting that took place on her soil, the second war did not have the destructive consequences of the first.

Nevertheless, France was once again obliged to rebuild her economy, her housing and industrial plant, and her spirit in the 1950s and after. It was a slow process, despite assistance from the American Marshall Plan.

Marie-Catherine and Auguste Santerre remained distant from the drama and excitement of national politics. The tragedies of war came close to them, partly because their native region and lifelong home was northern France, across which the twentieth-century wars raged. They were so intent on work—one really begins to understand the meaning of "earning your bread" in her descriptions of labor—that politics broke into their consciousness only seldom. Mémé's experience and knowledge of politics was always mediated and indirect. It was her father who objected to state policy on church schools; her uncle who told the family about working conditions and worker dissatisfaction elsewhere. She does not mention the weavers' strikes we know occurred in Avesnes-les-Aubert. It was her husband, and later her son, who had to report for military service and be exempted. It was Auguste who had to manage the harvest when the other male laborers went to war in August 1914. It was he who later became a volunteer fireman and provided an opinion about Nazis and collaborators for her.

The memoir of this simple woman is not that of an actor in the public arena, but of an observer. This is a fair representation of most French women's lives at the time. To see her as actor, we must look to the intimate life of family and couple, to work and how she experienced it, and to the impact on the small scale—on the everyday lives of ordinary people—of large-scale political and economic structural change. Though buffeted by fortune, the integrity and strength of Mémé Santerre shine through.

LOUISE A. TILLY

Mémé Santerre

Chapter One

I was born on December 23, 1891. That night, my mother told me, a sharp, freezing wind swept our row of houses, stirring up clouds of powdery snow that stuck to the brick walls and blew in beneath the doors. My mother had gone to bed an hour earlier with the first pains of labor. She didn't get up again for nine days.

Papa had made the bed with the finer sheets they saved for births. The round Flemish stove hummed like an organ, loaded to the brim with briquettes made of a mixture of peat and coal dust. That little stove heated us and cooked our food. That evening, a big pot of water boiled on top. My father sat, waiting silently for the midwife, Fat Zulma, to arrive; she had brought my twelve brothers and sisters into the world before me.

On the table glittered a *roue de brouette,* a "barrow wheel," as we called hundred-sou[1] silver coins. It would soon go to the midwife. If all went well, she would also get a special treat. There was a cup of good, strong real coffee; my father would break an egg into it. This was the only time we ever had these two delicacies in the house. Other days, we drank chicory. And eggs? We never ate them.

The north wind, stronger than ever, blew the sawdust that covered the floor of the only room in our house. That room was kitchen, dining room, and bedroom. My father, who was fussy about convention, had managed to construct a little garret under the eaves above. There my three sisters and I were heaved up in the evening to sleep.

As my mother groaned in rhythm with the wind, Papa was seized with fear. That damned Zulma was going to miss the birth of the child! Suddenly, from the distance, howls, like cries of infinite desperation, could be heard. Wolves. . . . The door opened to a violent push. Icy air blew in, and the fat woman who was to bring me into the world entered.

My birth, they told me, was quickly accomplished. Zulma had plenty of experience. That evening, she again earned her coffee. She traveled around the village and neighboring *corons*² like ours, delivering babies. She had plenty of work; all the families had at least ten children.

I was quickly pushed out from my mother's womb and washed. Then the midwife swaddled me in a complicated and precise procedure. She said that this swaddling would prevent my becoming deformed. Next Maman was carefully cleaned. Zulma didn't like her clients to die giving birth; she was good at preventing infection.

Having completed her work, she sipped her coffee with egg yolk. She spoke of the howling outside, of the wolves that had fled the great Belgian forests because of the cold. They had come as far south as our village to sniff at the doors on the outskirts of isolated settlements.

Wolves: I heard them several times myself, and I still remember them. I must have been four or five years old. Papa didn't like their howling at all. He said that it made him think of poor people who might be lost in the country, in danger of being devoured. My sisters and I were very frightened; on those evenings, we hugged each other tightly in our little room.

For the moment, though, I was a nursling who needed a

name. Maman cried a lot. She was very disappointed in another daughter, the eleventh. My older brother consoled her. "Mother," he said, "she will be the crutch of your old age." They decided to name me Marie-Catherine, after her.

Being the youngest, I had the privilege of saying "Maman." My brother and sisters had been expected to say "Mother" and "Father." We all had to address our parents formally. That was the custom in our province. And in our *coron,* which was a group of ten houses, every family observed this custom.

I never disputed my parents' word, of course, either before or after my marriage. Even if my sisters and I had been sure that they were mistaken, we would never have dared to tell them so.

Thus I grew, breast-fed until I was seven months old. It was the only milk I tasted in my entire childhood, apart from some I was given a few times in school.

At the age of three, I, like the others, was given chicory, with a hunk of bread in the morning. At noon, it was boiled potatoes and white cheese which we spread on thick *tartines.*[3] My mother seasoned the cheese with salt and garlic. We could get a big bowlful for three sous. In the evening, we drank bowls of soup. Meat was reserved for Sundays, and not always then. We had a little boiled beef or beef liver or innards. Maman made stews that smelled very tempting.

She never bought meat at the butcher. It was too expensive. We waited for the village crier, Père François, to beat his drum in the square, announcing that a farmer was going to kill a cow and sell it at his farm the next morning. At dawn, the housewives from the *coron* went together to the farm. They wanted to see the butchering of the beast and not miss buying the choice pieces. The errand had to be done quickly: the men didn't like to have their wives away from home. They were needed in the cellar.

The house's cellar . . . It was a big half-dark room, lit only by several high windows. In it were the looms. Everyone in the village wove during the winter months for eighteen hours each day. Once I had finished my schooling, I too had "my" loom. (Being the youngest, I had the most opportunity to go to school, and I went for [four][4] years.) I was still so tiny when I first wove that I had to have wooden "skates" attached to my feet so I could reach the pedals. My legs were too short!

We got up at 4:00 in the morning, each day. We washed with water that came from the court fifty meters away, where a well served all the families in our *coron,* and dressed. Hop! we went down the ladder to the cellar, with its two coal-oil lamps. In the meantime, my mother lit the round stove that heated the main room. The stove had niches in its main section where we could warm our frozen feet when she called us, around 10:00, to come upstairs and get our "coffee." It was a long time to wait after waking before we got our hot drink, so it seemed delicious to us.

Even today—really—there is nothing better than the chicory of my memories. While we were weaving, Maman straightened the house, scoured the floor, scraped the table with a shard of glass, threw fresh sawdust on the tiles, and boiled potatoes. At the same time, she wound the yarn we would weave the next day onto bobbins that fit into our shuttles. My sisters and I wove linen cloth for handkerchiefs, which we rolled into bolts. My father, who was stronger and more skillful, made wider pieces of linen. These wide lengths of cloth were more difficult to manage, but much sought after at that time.

Come Saturday, we would run one at a time to the merchant's agent, a neighbor in the *coron.* We tried to waste as little time as possible. He would collect our completed work and pay us for it. My earliest memory is earning two francs a week. When my handkerchiefs were perfect, as I learned to make them, the boss gave me five sous for a tip. Later, I earned up to five francs a week. But I always ran home and gave the money to my mother. My sisters would go then, one after another, and finally Papa, to take their work and get their pay.

We couldn't make ends meet with these pitiful earnings. All winter long, we lived on credit. Only when we came back from the season in the country were we able to pay our bills. Each year we worked for six months on a farm in the Seine-Inférieure, far from home.

In my early years, my father baked his own bread in the common oven of the *coron*. We would go get a jug of liquid yeast at the neighboring brewery, and Papa bought his flour at the mill. What a treat it was when he baked! He beat the dough vigorously and let it rise. Then he kneaded it into enormous six-pound loaves that he pushed into the oven with a long spatula. We waited, like good children, for our customary treat. By the light of the flaming logs, we would see, through the open door, my father's face toward the oven. Then he would smile and take out some little round loaves which we called *flamiques*. These little loaves were bread just like the rest, but they were shaped like the pastries that we never had the money to buy. On special days, Maman put some onions on top. That was an extra treat. These were our only childhood "dessert." But they were the best.

I loved my father. During his lifetime, not one of us was physically punished. We respected him for his strict and honest ways. Alas, not all the heads of families in our *coron* were so respectable. The only luxury in which my father indulged was a pint of beer when he had had a good week—which was rare. He seldom even raised his voice. I never heard him speak rudely to my mother. He adored her. Yet he was a simple man, raised strictly by stepparents because he had lost his natural parents when he was a child.

Once, when he was in one of his rare talkative moods, he told us that he was glad that our childhood was not like his had been.

He was inflexible only when it came to religion. He revered priests and nuns. When they were expelled from France, he went into the streets and fought with the police. It seemed scandalous to him that the good nuns could be exiled.[5] "They do nothing but good for all the world." He spent four days in prison for having attacked a policeman. The term was short because our district deputy testified in his favor at the request of the village mayor, who respected him. Otherwise, he would have had to stay in jail longer.

Around noon, we came up from the cellar to eat potatoes and chunks of white cheese. The menu was always the same, except on Sundays, when we had meat. Next, my father made us spend a half-hour in the court getting a bit of fresh air. The cellar was really pretty unhealthy. Around 1:00, we would go back to the loom to weave until 4:00. Then we would get another bowl of chicory and go back down until 7:00, when we got soup. A half-hour later, we returned to our work until about 10:00.

No one had to tell us twice to go to bed. Before going to sleep, we always thanked God for His gifts. We would recite the Our Father out loud, just as we always said grace before eating what food we had. Even now, I'm faithful to the prayers that I've said all my life.

On Sundays, we were up before 7:00. My mother scrubbed each member of the family vigorously in a great tub of hot water with a brush and green soap. Then we put on our best clothes and went to mass at 8:00. I was proud, dressed in my blue dress and white linen bonnet. The priest, who was very old, was also very nice. He asked us to practice charity and to have courage.

We had plenty of courage. Charity was a little more difficult. Still, when it came to helping someone worse off than us, my parents never hesitated to contribute a few sous. They were ready to do without a bit the next week, in order to help the needy.

To do without: what did that mean anyway? We never felt deprived of necessities. Only later, much later, did I realize exactly how many flavors and forms I had never known.

Fruits, for example. We never had them. They were too expensive. We never had as much as an apple. Sometimes on Christmas we got an orange, which we called the "fruit of paradise," its flavor was so unusual and exquisite to us.

We worked on Christmas like any other day. But there was a surprise in our thread boxes by the looms: a little Jesus made of spice cake. We nibbled at that for hours to prolong our pleasure. On Christmas Eve, we went to bed late, very late.

Before that, when the bells pealed, we had dressed warmly and gone in the snow and cold to the church, for midnight mass.

"It's the Nativity, children. You should never miss it," Papa said.

That mass was beautiful. It was warm in the choir, where many candles glowed. We stepped up to see the crèche where a baby was sleeping in the midst of the sheep, cows, and goats that the farmers brought to the church.

Our parents dragged us home; we were thrilled by what we had seen, but exhausted. Maman heated up a little chicory. That did us good.

After the perfume of incense in the church, I was struck on returning home by the flat odors that floated in the common room. There was a permanent smell, even in the cleanest houses. It still sticks in my memory. It was the smell of the peat that burned with the coal dust in the round stove. It caught in my throat sometimes and, amazingly enough, brought tears to my eyes. Whenever I smelled it, I was happy, perfectly happy.

One day, my father rushed back to the house from the

communal oven where he had gone to bake our bread. His face was white.

"It's a disaster, Marie-Catherine," he said to Maman. "The oven has fallen apart!"

This really was awful news. Maman turned very pale. "My God, what will become of us? What will you do, Pierre?"

My father stood there, dumbly, his jug of yeast and his bowl of dough in his hands. Throughout the neighborhood, people talked about the disaster. A delegation went to the owner of the oven. He sent everyone away, claiming he didn't have enough money to fix it.

"Look, men, I can't rebuild that oven with the hundred sous per month that you pay to use it. Clear out now!"

They left. Papa baked his bread that day in the oven of a farmer whom he knew slightly. It was the last time he made his own bread. When he came home that evening, he declared that we would have to buy our loaves from the baker from then on. "But that's impossible," said Maman. "A loaf costs eighteen sous, and we need one almost every day!"

The next day, Papa went to see the baker, Arsène. Arsène, a large man who was always dusted white with flour, wasn't a bad sort. But of course he had to be paid for his bread. "So," Papa told us later, "he proposed a *taille*."[6]

A *taille*? I didn't know what that meant. When I saw the relief on Maman's face, I realized that it must be something good. It was, sort of. It meant that Arsène would give us credit until our return from the country after the summer. He trusted my father, and his confidence was never betrayed. We had bread every day with this deal. When we went to pick up the six-pound loaf, we brought along our stick. Arsène's wife made a notch in it. Then she took her stick with our name carved in it and marked it the same way. When we returned in October, we would pay as many times eighteen sous as there were notches in the sticks.

The grocer had a notebook for his accounts. He marked

down the salt, sugar, chicory, lard—everything that we bought. We settled our account there, too, when we returned from the country.

My mother bought only clothes (our aprons, our hats, our dresses) and peat, which was sold in blocks. This served as fuel for the stove, mixed with the coal dust that Papa bought cheap from a far-off mine. "It's worth the trouble," he said. "The coal merchants are robbers."

Papa was very opinionated; he never changed his mind about some things. Sometimes he didn't have time to go get coal dust at the slag heap, and we had to buy real coal. As for me, I liked it when we burned coal, because then the house would not have that lingering smell. For some reason, it made me think of death.

Death had prowled in our house many years earlier, before I was born. Maman told me the story when I asked about the two sisters and the brother who were missing from our family.

"The story begins twenty-seven years ago, Marie. During the war of 1870. Your brother and your two sisters and I were left alone in the war. We were even worse off than we are nowadays. The emperor was in power at the time. We had work, but it paid so poorly that sometimes we had no bread. One day, we heard that there was a war—Papa had to be a soldier. He went to Cambrai, and I was on my own."

My mother's voice trembled when she recalled this time. I told her to stop, that I didn't want to hear the story. But she continued, saying that I ought to know.

"I couldn't care for your brother because I had to weave. A kind neighbor took care of him. She didn't have any children and was eager to have him. My poor baby! One night, the neighbor came in screaming. She had just knocked a basin of boiling water on the child! He died the next day. He was buried without a coffin, like a dog in the earth. I couldn't afford anything more, and your father wasn't told about it at the time. He didn't find out about his son's death until later, when he returned from the fighting."

It was awful to hear how the little brother—whom I didn't know and never would know—had died. However, the worst of the story was yet to come.

"Your two sisters got ill," continued my mother in a quavering voice. "The doctor came only once. He said that they needed meat broth or they would die. I didn't see him again. It was the mayor who came to register their deaths. They died calmly, quietly. I gave them my breast at the end to soothe them, but I didn't have any milk. I was pregnant with your sister Louise.

"Papa couldn't get leave when he finally heard of his triple loss. There was a battle at Sedan; no soldiers were allowed on leave. So he left everything—his barracks, his gun. He ran away in the night to return home.

"He rushed into the house one evening," Maman told me, "acting like a madman. I was penniless. He swore that he wouldn't leave again until he had woven a large piece of linen. I could then live for several weeks, until the birth of your sister, with the money from selling the cloth.

"The police came to get him. They had a long chain with which they intended to lead him behind their horse. They went down into the cellar and were astounded when they saw your father weaving! He told them he wouldn't leave his loom until he had finished the cloth, and I tried to explain our plight to them too.

" 'Well,' said the one who had three stripes, 'I think you are a good man. Stay here. Promise me that you will go back as soon as you have finished.' Papa gave his word. He did rejoin the Cambrai regiment as he had promised. The police had written the commander, so he was never punished."

Maman talked for a long time about that awful period, which was one long stretch of bad luck. Father was a prisoner of the Prussians on an island near Sedan, eventually escaping from the troops that swarmed over the region. I loved my parents all the more for their endurance of these troubles.

They suffered more than you can imagine. Yet they were always happy because, I know, they adored each other. Just as I too adored my husband. They didn't know how to read or write, they had no contact with the outside world. The radio was unknown, of course; newspapers were expensive, and you had to be able to read to understand them. Nevertheless, they were both intelligent, sensible, and kind. Their kindness toward us children was endless.

After I learned how my older sisters died, I didn't dare grumble or complain. When I had bread to eat, I was satisfied. As Papa said, there were lots of children who had nothing! Before each humble meal, we sincerely thanked God for providing it.

On my sixth birthday, Mama kissed me, as she always did on that day. She told me that I was going to go to school. There had been a family council between my parents about this decision.

"The others didn't go to school," said Papa. "She is the last, we should do more for her. She should at least learn the alphabet and the multiplication tables."

I went to class at the convent school for the first time on the day after Christmas. The nuns had been replaced by the ladies from the château, who taught the classes. Papa hadn't hesitated in choosing this school. He rejected the communal school out of hand. We called it the "corner school."

Each family in the village sent their children to one school or the other, depending on their political and religious convictions. The total number of children was small, so it was easy to figure out everyone's opinions.

At the convent school, we had ten students; there were five or six at the other. We didn't mix with them, even after school. On the common, the grassy square near the church, we each played on our own side. The students of the convent were put at the head of the line when we all received first communion.

We did a little mathematics and some reading, and we learned our catechism. I liked my school very much. It was in a warm part of the parsonage, and the ladies from the château were very nice. Sometimes they gave us a little milk. The winter passed like that. When spring came and we left Avesnes for the country, Papa, like the other heads of families that "migrated," contacted the parochial school in our neighborhood in the Seine-Inférieur, and I continued my studies there. [7]

This went on for four years. They were the best years of my childhood. Then one day my father announced that I knew enough and that I would have to work at a loom like my two sisters.

That was the end of my lazy mornings. No more sleeping until 7:00. I began my difficult apprenticeship when I was only knee-high to a grasshopper. For eight years, and after, when I was married, I took my place in the big cellar, which was only dimly lit by coal-oil lamps. Later, these were replaced with kerosene lamps.

In the cellar there were four looms, two on one side and two on the other. The big one was reserved for Papa; my sisters and I worked on the three smaller ones.

My sisters Emérance and Anatolie were the only ones still at home. My brother Léandre and all the others were married. Their names were Louise, Zulma, Palmyre, Lucie, Edwige, Espérance.

Lucie lived in the same village as us. I never saw the others. [8] They were scattered around the region, married to seasonal workers. The poor women never had time to themselves. Pour souls, they rarely visited. After the war, they scattered even farther, so I never saw any of them again. Every now and then, word came that one of them had died. Being twenty years younger, I never knew them well.

So my childhood years passed, filled with the simple joys of family. The only high point of those years was the day of my first communion. It was a day like any other, but so beautiful that I can still remember it.

My godfather came just before the mass. He brought me a little apron; my godmother gave me a piece of material for a dress. They put a white veil on my head and gave me a candle, a big gilt candle. I was allowed to hold it for a few moments, only for the procession. After the ceremony, we returned home and Papa offered beer to everyone. The veil, which had already been used by my sisters and was later to be used by my nieces, was carefully folded and placed in the cupboard, wrapped up in tissue paper. Then we went down into the cellar to weave until it was time for vespers.

After vespers, my mother let me wear my new apron. That was the greatest thrill of the day. I was eleven years old. It was June 1901, just before our departure for the country.

Chapter Two

As the winter drew to a close, our long days in the cellar grew more and more difficult to endure. My sisters and I, especially, with my short legs, had a hard time pushing the pedals that moved the sheds of our loom. When it was time to go to sleep, around 10:00 in the evening, Papa often had to carry me to bed in his arms. I couldn't bend over my work anymore, and I barely had the energy to swallow my hot chicory. We slept like logs, but my exhausted legs still ached when I got up the next morning.

Papa sang to encourage us during these last weeks. He had a fine voice, but he liked to make us ask before he'd begin. It took a little clowning with my sisters before he'd start singing. We would be complaining more than we should. Then my father would say, "Ah! you little loafers, you hear me sing too much. Come on, be lively, for goodness' sake! We won't make money this week unless you work harder than you are now. Come on . . . come on . . . be brave. Look, my little ones, I will sing you a song."

Finally, he would start. I remember well. His songs were very beautiful. There was the one that Papa liked best, maybe because of the title: "The Dream Weavers." I haven't heard it since, except once after the war. It went like this:

> *Babies' dreams are woven of white silk,*
> *They draw their life from their mother's bountiful breast,*
> *Their little fingers squeeze until their thirst is quenched,*
> *Then they close their big eyes on sweet dreams.*

And then he sang "In Cherry Time." Papa said that the author, whose first name, I remember, was Jean-Baptiste,* like the husband of one of my sisters, was a "boar" like him—a native of the Ardennes and its thick forests.

One passage especially struck me: "The pretty girls' heads were full of madness." That bothered me. I wondered why the beauties went mad, and I asked my father, who answered me, laughing: "You'll know soon enough." That stopped my questioning. But the song that my sisters and I preferred above all was the one about the lilacs:

> *When the lilacs bloom,*
> *We will wear woolen hoods*
> *And red dresses against the wind.*
> *When the lilacs bloom,*
> *We will dance in rings*
> *On the green carpet of the fields.*
> *When the lilacs bloom,*
> *Tell spring that it is time.*

We waited impatiently for the coming of warmer weather and our departure for the country. Then we too would "dance in rings" in one of the big fields where we would spend more than six months of the year.

Our round of life was cut into two parts. It wasn't that the

---

*Jean-Baptiste Clément.

life in the country that we so looked forward to was much more pleasant than that which we lived in the winter. We waited impatiently for summer because then we would be outdoors.

It was a long trip to the department of the Seine-Inférieure, where we went to work. We paid four francs each for the train, and I remember we changed at least twice on the way.

People often ask why we didn't stay and work on the farms in the region where we lived. It was impossible, because the farms there weren't big enough. Near Avesnes, the properties were tiny; they had been subdivided many times, and the farmers could barely live on what they grew. The proof was that every now and then they had to slaughter an animal, butcher it, and sell it in order to make ends meet.

Because there was no work closer to home, we had to emigrate in the month of May. For us kids, the move to new horizons was a joy, but for my parents, what a pain! They had to pack our baggage. Each of us had a bundle of clothes, larger or smaller depending on the size of its owner. Papa and Maman were weighed down like donkeys. Maman hid a little gray purse in her corset, in which she kept the family money. She rarely had more than three or four francs left after we paid for the railroad tickets. Sometimes we had to borrow to pay for the tickets and send a money order when the farm at Saint-Martin reimbursed us for our voyage, which was part of the deal.

We were very eager to breathe the fresh air of the country, but we still had heavy hearts when it came to leaving our own little cottage. Before our departure, we always cleaned it from top to bottom. The straw mattresses were folded, the stove carefully scrubbed, ready to get back to work on our return, and the briquettes of coal dust and peat were piled up to the ceiling. They dried there all summer long in the empty main room.

You could hear the clatter of the looms until the day before our departure. We had to hurry in order to finish and deliver the bolts of cloth. Quickly, quickly!

At 5:00 the next morning, everyone jumped eagerly out of bed, in our house and every other house in the *coron*. All the families left together, or almost together, for the big farms in Normandy. They were expected. Most of them—families like ours that were serious and hard-working—returned to the same farm year after year. In those days we didn't bother with the paperwork that people do today. A person's word was as good as a signed contract. Of course, under these conditions we couldn't be too particular about our pay. But sometimes we managed to get a little more money for a little less work.

There would be a long procession of us walking to the nearest railroad station, which was at Cambrai, twelve kilometers away. Every morning, a horse-drawn cab, which we called "the mail," would go by, but it cost too much. Papa said, "When you're lucky enough to have good legs, you ought to know how to use them. Carriages are for the rich, my little ones; walking will give you round calves so you will find good husbands more quickly."

So we walked with our bundles on the ends of sticks, and it seemed a long, long time before we could see the clock tower of the town in the distance. When we finally arrived, we settled in the railroad-station waiting room and devoured two hunks of bread that my mother had spread with plenty of fresh white cheese. This was washed down with a cup of clear water dipped from the station's fountain in the freight room. Then the train would come puffing in. Each father would settle his brood as best he could. As we pulled out of the station, our heads instinctively turned back toward our village, already far behind. Our feelings were divided between our anticipated joys in the country and the sorrow of leaving home.

Avay was a village in the Seine-Inférieure with houses clustered around its church and cemetery.[1] The Saint-Martin farm where we were going to work was about a kilometer from the village. We were thankful that it wasn't farther, because we had to attend mass and vespers there on Sunday. During the harvest or the sugar-beet–picking season, we sometimes missed church when our work was pressing. The priest told my father that we were excused, for God preferred strong people who missed mass because of their work to those weaklings who went because they didn't know how to use the ten fingers He gave them. Nevertheless, Papa hated not being able to go to church on Sunday. "It seems like I'm missing something to make my joy complete," he would say to Maman.

The Saint-Martin farm was large, very large. As I grew up, it seemed to shrink in my eyes. I know that it wasn't the farm shrinking; it was me growing. I've often noticed that when we see the places where we lived as children later in life, they seem different. One thinks that they have changed; really, it's not they, it's we who have changed.

As soon as we got out of the four-wheeled carts that met us at the Dieppe railroad station, we had to move into the lodgings that were assigned to us. We would live there for the next months. Our home was smaller than the one in Avesnes. The beds were squeezed one against the other because each family lived in a single room. Sometimes there was a wood stove; sometimes a fireplace. Maman always went directly to that part of the room, because it was "hers." There she would cook the vegetables for our meals. We had to buy these vegetables, in addition to bread and cheese. The farmers gave us bowls of a good thick soup made from meat at noon and in the evening. Sometimes we even found little pieces of meat in the soup. They were good but, unfortunately, we didn't find them very often.

Before my marriage, five of us worked: my father, my mother, my sisters Emérance and Anatolie, and I. Other families had more workers. Seven or eight children would go to the fields, even the little ones. Papa said it was shameful to put five- or six-year-olds to work. "There is a time for everything in life," he explained. "Just because a father was forced to work with kicks on the behind at an early age, he shouldn't do the same to his little kids." In our family, we waited until we were eleven, because he said that that was quite young enough.

The Saint-Martin farm produced only wheat and sugar beets. It belonged to a big company in Paris which owned many farms throughout France. We only saw the agent, who wasn't a bad sort. Anyway, for most of the work, it didn't matter. We were paid by the job, for example, for the wheat harvest. The more one did, the more one got. And each person in a family had to work his own assigned plot of ground. We were paid by the row for thinning the sugar beets and by the pound for the harvest. Wheat was toted up in bales, made up of two sheaves. We were paid by the day only for working in the farmyard or house and for spreading night soil.

We received our entire pay when we left in November. It was a substantial amount of money, as much as we ever saw at one time. In some seasons, we had to ask for small advances in order to pay for our vegetables, bread, and lard. Families that liked fancy living got many advances, so they didn't receive much when they left. "When one drinks wine, when one smokes, you can't make it," said Papa. "Also, you must have the luck of marrying a thrifty wife, which is rare," he added. Maman blushed under her piped bonnet at this indirect compliment, one of the few he paid her.

That year, like all the others, we moved in and started to work the very next day at 6:00 A.M. I could never believe the extent of the fields, which seemed to spread on forever. At the beginning of May, they were covered with fine green sprouts. Wheat fields undulated in the distance. These were the fields that we would keep free from thistles. We sliced through the thistles with one clean blow of the hoe; they would ooze a greenish milk from their sliced stalks. "That's good for colic," Maman said.

Marcel, the surveyor, would arrive at the same time as we, with a clinking of rods against his hundred-meter iron chain. He surveyed each plot of the field to be harvested. When we had finished our plot, three, four, or five days later, the agent would inspect to see that the work was done thoroughly and to record the number of the field and plot. Then we knew that we had earned forty sous. But we had to have all the pricklers killed. If one thistle was still standing, the agent complained loudly.

In some families, he was called "the big squealer." I noticed that he hardly said anything when inspecting our plots. There was never a thistle left. That was because Papa made us understand that no matter what we did, we had to do it well. No doubt it's because of this that the company employed my parents, and later me and my husband, all our lives, with no complaints about any of us. Still, this sort of work was hard for a little girl! When I saw the plot I was assigned, it seemed as if I would never reach the end of those long, long rows.

Once we got to the end of a row, we had to turn right away, without standing up. From time to time I stopped to look at a bird or to observe a motionless toad in front of me, staring at me with gold-circled eyes. The toads bothered me. It seemed that they were there to watch me. But Papa didn't tolerate daydreams. He would bring me back to reality. "Your sister will finish her plot before you if you laze about like that all the time," he would yell. He didn't say it meanly and his tone was never angry. He just said it, but that was enough to get my hoe moving again, chopping each green thistle with one clean blow.

Around 10:00 A.M., everyone stopped for a bit. From our smock pockets we would pull out pieces of bread, spread with the cheese Maman made from the whey the farm sold her. A mouthful of warm chicory, drunk from Papa's canteen to wash it down, and we resumed work until noon. Heat or rain never stopped our work unless it rained extremely hard or there was a thunderstorm.

Peasants don't like thunderstorms. To them, lightning and thunder accompanied by a downpour that ruins the harvest are signs of the heavens' fury. They don't like to brave such storms.

My father had a deep fear of thunder, and at the first clap he made us immediately drop all metal tools and run for shelter. His father was killed while reaping in a thunderstorm. A long blue arc of electricity had touched the keen edge of his blade. It was as though the lightning had killed Grandpa for having defied the storm. All they found of him was a few ashes and his blackened sabots. Every year, Papa told this story to the other workers, who were terrified.

So, as soon as it thundered, there was panic. The company agents didn't say anything when work was interrupted like that. They had had workers killed by lightning and it cost them a lot. They had to give money to the widow—maybe fifty francs, we heard.

After chopping out the thistles, a job which lasted to the end of May, we had to remove rocks from the same wheat fields where we had spent the preceding weeks. The stones that threatened to dull the sharp blades of the scythes had to be picked out of the earth. We placed them in baskets that we carried on our backs and emptied into the nearby roads. There they helped the oxcarts get through the mire of wet weather. This job, too, was long, tiring, and monotonous. When we reached the end of the field, the road was far off and we had to jump over the furrows, straining under the weight of the basket, to avoid crushing the tender, green shoots. We dared not trample the shoots! We knew that in August they would be big stalks heavy with grain that was made into flour and then bread. And bread was precious and good.

Gathering the stones was poorly paid, exhausting work, but

my sisters and I weren't in a hurry, because what followed was even worse. Papa wasn't that cheerful either when he announced in the evening, "Tomorrow, my little ones, we begin spreading fertilizer." The fertilizer, what a nightmare! Of all the things I've had to do in my life, none took so much out of me. The oxcarts would arrive in a long parade, beginning early in the morning—slowly but surely. They had left in the night for the railroad station at Dieppe, where night soil would arrive by the carload. The oxen would stolidly pull them to the fields where we would be waiting for them. Once there, they turned off the road and, with their necks extended and eyes bulging out of their heads, pulled their heavy loads into the cultivated fields. Their drovers spurred them on by yelling, "Ah oua, my big Clairon! Come on, dia Alexandre, my good beast!"

The carter would quickly pull out the pin and release the wooden bar so that the dump wagon could tip its evil-smelling contents into an enormous pile that it seemed we could never finish spreading. It had to be spread with pitchforks. The whole family worked together on this job. That way, each cartful was spread out more quickly.

When we returned, exhausted, we still had to face the ordeal of the pump. Maman washed us with green soap right in the trough to remove the long dirty streaks from our short legs. Despite this scrubbing, our evening soup didn't taste very good. An awful odor of spoilage, of rot, stuck to us. It still filled our nostrils long after we had finished that foul task.

When it was done, Papa would say to Maman, "Well, Marie-Catherine, we worked hard; with the manure-spreading we will pay the baker's accounts when we return." In fact, we did earn more for manure-spreading, so we were satisfied that we were helping pay for the six-pound loaves.

Those evenings, while he washed himself in a big tub behind a curtain sewn out of two sacks, Papa would sing at the top of his lungs:

When cherry time comes,
The nightingales and the starlings
All celebrate gaily . . .

Joyfully, we breathed the fresh country air again, even though what came next was no vacation either. For now it was time to thin the sugar beets. There were long, long furrows, where we left only the most robust and best-centered plants so that the finished row would be straight as an *I*. Each row brought us three sous. One could do up to four in a day, but only without dawdling to look at the flies along the way! We worked bent over the furrow, with one foot on either side, our short-handled hoe constantly digging into the soil. The victims of the thinning, little plants that were spindly or less well placed than the others, were tossed to one side or the other.

I found a way to distract myself: I counted to ten five times before stretching. But the first days were still hard. I felt as if someone were tearing out my kidneys with big tweezers or as though a red-hot iron burned in my back. That lasted a week; then my body got used to its forced gymnastics. In the evening, we spread out on our mattresses of fresh straw; we fell into bed as though made of lead, heavily, aching, unable even to take off our clothes.

Then Papa or Maman would come with a bowl of soup, lift our heads gently, and feed us the hot soup from a spoon. How good that soup was on those evenings! Our parents' tenderness filled us with great joy, and after prayers we slept huddled together, happy and satiated.

Just as the sun grew more and more bright at dawn, as the blue sky seemed warmer and warmer by 10:00, so harvest time came closer, day by day.

A couple of days before the harvest, strapping, hairy men arrived at the farm, talking and laughing loudly: they were the reapers, come from Flanders, with their scythe blades, gleaming like silver, in their sacks.[2] They would sharpen them with sweeping strokes against the whetstones which they soaked in horns full of water attached to their waists. They brought not only their blades, but also the wooden handles which shone like waxed furniture, worn smooth by their hands.

One of the reapers explained to Papa that these tools were precious. Without his own scythe, the best reaper was clumsy. By balancing his tool, before beginning, he could find the curve in the wood that the left hand melded to, while the fingers of the right hand fit into the little indentations that hours of work had worn.

We were always a bit scandalized by the life of the reapers, always ready with an off-color joke. The seasonal laborers didn't like to leave their wives and daughters alone for long when the reapers were around, for fear they would prowl into the farmyard. At the farm, they all lived in the same barn, sleeping in the straw. In the morning, they would sing while they washed and shaved at the pump, splashing themselves with water. They sang a lot and ate as much. The farm fed them, and we were stunned to see how much they ate at a single meal.

In the morning, they had large bowls of coffee and milk with bread and cheese when they rose. At 8:00, they had a thick, boiling soup; then, at 10:00, small loaves of bread and meat washed down with beer. At 1:00, their lunch would consist of salt pork, boiled potatoes, an enormous quantity of cheese, and a pot of steaming coffee. In the afternoon, around 3:00, they returned to the farm for big loaves of bread sliced into enormous salad bowls of raw milk. And at 10:00 P.M., when work ended, they dined—with meat, eggs, and broth this time. It looked like an orgy to us, who were not used to such quantities of food!

But reaping was grueling and difficult work. The farmers

paid well because, as they said, "a good reaper is not easy to find." Those big, laughing, blond men were solid as rocks. In the evenings after dinner, as they smoked their pipes in the farmyard, they still had the strength to sing the songs of their homeland in rough and joyous voices.

My father respected the reapers. He admired their spirit, although he himself was no sloucher, of course. His only reservation was that they were too inclined to fool around with women. He never approved of that.

Although they went to bed late, they were up promptly and faithfully at their posts the next day. Lined up in rows like a battle formation, they were ready to go as the skies brightened after dawn. At the signal of the foreman, they began to cut the golden waves of wheat. Their scythes flashed in front of them like shining dancers; as they sliced the stems, there was an odd, whistling sound. They stopped from time to time; the whetstones resonated clearly on the metal that each reaper honed in his own way. Then the ballet would continue, the sharpened scythes whistling even more beautifully, continuing their work among the heavy golden stalks.

Ah, the reapers! I missed them when they left never to return. They were replaced by the enormous mechanical beast that arrived in later years. It did the work of ten reapers. But it didn't sing! When I walked behind the machine, I was deafened by the noise of the knives coming and going and nauseated by the smell of the gasoline that the driver poured into the green-painted flanks of his machine.

For the moment, though, we seasonal laborers followed the reapers across the long fields of wheat. Sometimes "mine"— the one who preceded me—would turn toward me after sharpening his blade and smile under his blond mustache. "*Godfordom!* You aren't very big for this sort of work!"

And it seemed that he sometimes went more slowly on purpose in order to give me time to catch up. I gathered all the

wheat that he cut into big armfuls, which were called sheaves.
With two sheaves we made a bale, which we tied together and
dragged to a stack where the wheat dried.

We worked quickly in order to avoid being outdistanced by
the great devils moving so swiftly ahead of us with the whistling, crunching sound of the blade on the wheat. When I
could overtake "my" reaper, I was very pleased. I played a
game that flattered me. I wasn't tall or well-rounded for my
thirteen years, but I imagined that, if he slowed down, it was
because he was in love with me! The poor man! No doubt his
thoughts were far from that sort, but this little romance made
my work less tedious. Sometimes I got so close to him that I
smelled the strong odor of sweat from his naked and muscle-
knotted torso. When I stopped for a breath, I watched his
muscles ripple with the movement of the scythe, in perfect
harmony with the tool. Then suddenly, ashamed of watching
him like that, I would blush and bend quickly to gather the
wheat. Later, I understood that these feelings foreshadowed a
change that occurred that year.

One morning when I awoke, I found myself covered with
blood. Frightened, I called my mother. I thought that I was
sick and had gotten a hernia because of my exertions. Maman
had a lot of trouble reassuring me. "It happens regularly to
your older sisters and me," she told me. But I didn't want to
believe it. So, for the first time, she explained a secret that
until then I hadn't understood.

"You know that each month your Papa doesn't sleep in bed
for a few days, but on the floor, rolled up in a blanket." That
had often intrigued me, but Papa had said that sleeping on the
floor was good for his rheumatism. "When your father sleeps
like that, it is because I am as you are today," added Maman.
"And this will happen to you every month unless you are
expecting a baby."

All this was not very clear in my young head, but I finally

let myself be convinced. Besides, I realized that it wasn't all that bad, because they let me stay in bed all day for that first time. It was during the sugar-beet harvest and I remember that it was pouring rain. At first, I was content to stay indoors; then, as the sad and empty hours rolled by, I felt ashamed to be spoiled like that, with Papa having to do my work.

The sugar-beet harvest, like all the farm labor, was unpleasant, especially because bad weather was more frequent in September. We pulled up the beets by hand. The machines one sees nowadays that pull beets from the earth mechanically were unheard of then. We took them by the stem and then swung them to get up the momentum to throw them into the oxcarts that followed after us. A full day like that was exhausting, but it and the fertilizer-spreading were the best-paid jobs. Only when the weather was really bad did we stay back at the farm. The men would work in the farmyard, repairing and tinkering, and we kids would help in the stable or the kitchen.

When the beet harvest was finished, my parents went with the other grownups down to the sugar refinery at Avay to wash the beets and get them ready for pulping. The kids stayed at the farm, some helping with the laundry and others picking the vegetables for the meals of the many year-round farm workers. Each night Papa and Maman came back from the sugar refinery, exhausted by the work and by the walk, despite a shortcut through the woods by a rough path. They never said anything about it and they never complained; nevertheless, their faces were deeply etched by fatigue.

In the evening, by the light of the lamp that was needed by the end of our stay, they were even less talkative than usual, which is saying a lot. When I think back on my parents, it's probably that which surprises me most about them: the small number of words they spoke in a day.

Papa felt that words were often useless. Once he added, on a rare day when he expressed himself more fully, that it was hardly necessary on a rainy day to say, "It's raining." "That's a waste of my time. I know that it is raining, for God's sake! I'm not deaf or blind," he muttered.

When I see the way families chat together today, I am astonished. Children even talk while eating, which was strictly forbidden in our house once grace was said. To get bread or water, we raised our hands and lightly snapped our thumbs and forefingers.

At the end of November—we generally left on my saint's day, Saint Catherine's Day—the farm that had been so luxuriant in May had become sinister. Its long buildings were swept with a steady, sharp, freezing north wind. The fields were desolate. We went back to see them as we were leaving. The earth where we had labored was plowed into big black furrows; under the gray sky, the crows hopped clumsily in the fields. There was snow sometimes, a white immensity that covered everything—fields, walls, thickets, and road. The farm was transformed. In our lodgings, we had to economize on wood for the little stove. We were given five logs a day, and they were burned quickly. Luckily, our room wasn't big and we stayed warm enough together. Besides, we didn't stay up late. As soon as we had swallowed our soup, we went to bed. As he blew out the lamp, Papa always said that in the dark, as we could tell, we couldn't even see the color of our ideas.

So we were as happy to leave as we had been to arrive. Maman's cloth purse tucked into her corset would be full of the money we got the day before leaving. Then it was time to go to the agent to settle the accounts. He would call "Gardez family" and read off all that we had done. Papa, who could neither read nor write, had me mark down all our work in a little notebook as we went along. We had no quarrel with the foreman. His calculations were always the same as ours. Things didn't go as well with other families. There were men who never agreed with the agent, who accused him of robbing them. "It's you fellows who try to rob me!" he would declare.

In the background of all the talk, we heard an unfamiliar

sound. It was gold or silver pieces clinking from hand to hand and disappearing into purses or wallets. When the pay session started, the agent had piles of coins in front of him. As the families filed past, the piles shrank. They shrank until no more coins were left. When all the pay was distributed, we left to pack up our bundles of clothes.

The next morning at dawn, the wagons took everyone to the train station; we retraced the same voyage in the train as before, but this time in reverse. At the other end, the cottage and its cellar waited for us.

Chapter Three

That year, we returned to Avesnes in an awful snowstorm. It was 8:00 P.M. when the train arrived in Cambrai. The stationmaster, who knew us a little, warned us. The road was blocked with huge drifts of snow and, according to him, it wouldn't be smart to leave at such a late hour for a twelve-kilometer trip. He suggested that we sleep in the waiting room, where he would stoke the fire.

As snow drifted onto the tracks along the platform, there was a conference among all the heads of families. The big wood stove in the waiting room, white-hot, was cozy and appealing, and some were for staying there until the storm passed. Others wanted to leave, for fear that overnight it would become even more difficult to travel and it would be impossible to return home the next day. When Papa was consulted, he allowed that he didn't know what to do. In the end, those who wanted to leave carried the day and our band set off into the white night.

What an awful trip! The memory is as clear as if it were yesterday that it happened.

While we were still protected by the tall brick buildings in the streets of Cambrai, it wasn't so bad. But once past the brewery, the open fields of Troupeaux stretched before us. The whirling snow seized us, penetrating our clothes with big, cold flakes. With no barrier for kilometers, the wind howled and seemed to gallop, blowing clouds of icy powder. Children began to cry, thinking they had seen wolves. Men swore in God's name, something they seldom did. Our pitiful band pushed on through all this, intent on reaching our *coron*, still so far away. My kerchief was soaked and my eyes were full of tears. My fingers, which Maman had wrapped in coarse woolen stockings, were frozen stiff around the stick carrying my bundle of belongings.

"It's a joke anyway, this filthy snow that keeps coming!" yelled someone next to me. As if in response to this insult, the storm increased in fury. Luckily, the snowplow had already passed down the road, so we only sank in up to our ankles. We pushed on like this, walking in the footsteps of those who went first, heads down, huddled as much as possible in order to offer the least possible body surface to the piercing cold.

How long did this nightmare go on? I don't know, but I can't forget it. Years—really years—passed before my legs felt warm again. That dreadful blizzard had frozen my bones for the rest of my life.

It was very late when we arrived in Avesnes. I no longer knew where I was, bewildered, blinded, my face turned raw by the north wind, my hands blue with cold, my clothes soaked. Our *coron*, buried under a meter of snow, was silent, its windows black. Our cottages were there, dark, but waiting faithfully.

Sinking in to our thighs, we all eagerly rushed toward the closed doors. Then came the sound of keys turning in the big iron locks over the raging blast of the wind, which seemed to regret the sight of us escaping it.

Papa pushed our door open, knocking big clumps of snow off his galoshes. "Praise God, we're home! That's not so bad!"

His beard was white, covered with little balls of ice, and to see him like that—believe it or not—made us laugh. As soon as we came into the shelter, we were much warmer, away from the infernal sound of the icy wind, and the kerosene lamp, quickly lit, showed us the familiar room, unchanged. It was even dearer to me because I had been afraid that I would never see it again. Papa went right to the woodchest and, using the paper in which the sugar and chicory had been wrapped before our departure, lit a fire. The little Flemish stove, its chimney surrounded by the whirling winds outside, set to work.

We took off our soaked clothes and, wrapped up in bed-clothes, shivered around the fire. "Ah," said Maman with a sigh, holding her hands toward the stove, "it feels good to be home."

Papa rummaged in the cellar. He had opened the trap door and gone down the ladder right away to look around. We heard the sheds of each loom go up and down, one after another.

Although we were overcome with fatigue, we stayed there, snuggled up with well-being, watching our clothes begin to steam in the stove's heat. Miraculously, there also was the good odor of chicory tickling our nostrils. Maman indulged us and Papa showed his approval in smiling silence. We drank our hot, sugared drink slowly. I felt Papa's arm hug me clumsily. I felt warm and good as I fell asleep.

The next day, we didn't get back to our work until the afternoon. By 8:00, Papa had left to pay Arsène's bill and our account at the grocer. "First as usual, Gardez. You are a good risk," they said. From Arsène's shop he brought us a *flamique*, the little round loaf, and three pieces of sugar candy from the grocer, rewards for good customers.

The storm hadn't yet ended, thus supporting the argument of those who had insisted on our return the night before. The *coron* came back to life. Even though no one went far, each chimney belched forth thick white clouds from burning peat and coal dust. After our soup, we went back to work. My legs remembered the rhythm right away, as soon as I began to weave cloth for handkerchiefs with the shuttles that Maman prepared.

I was fourteen the next month, and that year I began "stealing" cloth from Maman. Oh, it wasn't wicked; I did it with her consent, as my sisters had before me. At the end of a length, instead of giving her the leftover thread, we saved it to make handkerchiefs for our trousseaux. Although they had no other linen when they married, the girls from our *coron* always had lots of handkerchiefs.

Knowing that I, like my sisters, had begun this petty thievery, my father pretended to be angry. "Ah! The scoundrel! She doesn't leave us enough to make a dish towel. Her trousseau! I ask you, who has ever told such a farfetched tale? You poke her nose and milk still comes out. And this kid thinks about marrying!" But he was talking through his beard; every now and then I found a beautiful little linen napkin in my thread basket. Papa too had "stolen" from Maman.

The uneventful years of my adolescence passed. Winter in the cellar, summer in the country; nothing interrupted our never-ending work, our same daily routines. The family was happy like that; we didn't envy others, and for a good reason: we didn't know any other way of life. The inhabitants of the *coron* never talked among themselves except about events in their own lives.

"Louise has had a little one. Fat Zulma was there last night." Or, "Poor Mathilde died this morning. She surely suffered a lot." And the neighboring women went on with their tasks; only the end differed according to the event. Either one would see the midwife run by or four men would go past, bearing the black stretcher with its four silver knobs, for the coffin.

Sickness was even more of a disaster than death, about

which, alas, one could do nothing. Sickness threw whole families into despair in no time. In our family—it was extraordinary but true—I never saw anyone seriously ill. We had colds, flu, muscle sprains like everyone else, sure, but we never called the doctor for these little problems. Maman often collected herbs in the countryside, plants that she alone knew. She stored them in little bags made of cloth. And each time one of us felt sick, she would make herb tea, which made us feel better right away. Grippe, cough, colic could be cured with these little linen sachets. My mother said that there was only one disease she couldn't cure with her plants: it was hunger.

Just after I turned sixteen, we had an unexpected visitor. It was Christmas 1907, a dry day, with a clear, cold sky. We had returned from mass and Maman was preparing the soup when we heard cartwheels crunching the pebbles in the road. "Why, it's Sulphart!" Maman, who had looked out the window, cried happily.

Uncle Sulphart, her brother. I couldn't believe my ears. I had often heard tell of him. He was the family adventurer. He wandered the roads of France with his cart, pulled by a donkey. He was a peddler, and we had been told that his vehicle contained a thousand and one marvels that he sold all over the country. Along with Zéphyrin, his donkey, he had a dog, Gros Loup [Fat Wolf]. When evening came, he would fold up his wares and sleep in his wagon, no matter what the weather was like, unless a generous farmer invited him to stay.

Uncle Sulphart! It had been many years since his tour of France had brought him to Avesnes. I didn't remember ever having seen him, so he couldn't have come for a long time. My sisters and I clapped our hands with joy. Our uncle entered, dressed in a long robe of bleached wool. In his hand, he held his soft leather hat and a sack made out of jute. Then there were hugs and compliments all around; they seemed like

they would never end. Uncle Sulphart brought news of the
family, news he had collected on his trip.

There was great excitement when he opened his sack and
took out presents for each of us: multicolored scarves for Maman, my sisters, and me; a corduroy cap for Papa. And, for an
extra surprise, we got little silver medallions with the Virgin
Mary's face. I've kept mine ever since. My medal is worn thin
nowadays, but I still hold it between my fingers and think
back on my youth and about my husband, whom I gave the
medal to.

After hours of talk, our uncle began to worry about shelter
for Zéphyrin. We lodged him under the baker's lean-to, after
feeding him a nosebag full of bread scraps furnished by
Arsène. It was an unbroken tradition that Uncle Sulphart
wouldn't take a bite to eat himself until he saw his donkey
feeding and wiggling his ears with satisfaction. Then he would
cover the donkey with a thick leather blanket lined with
wool. With his big cloth kneepads and the shining hide of a
well-cared-for beast, Zéphyrin was sheltered from aches or
cold.

Then Uncle, satisfied, returned to the house, without his
donkey but with Gros Loup at his heels. What a surprise—a
real miracle! There, on the round stove, something that
smelled delicious was frying. It was big pieces of bacon that
Papa had hurried out to buy, along with two pints of beer.
What a party there was around the table! Bacon, pickled
cabbage, and the uncle who told story after story. We listened
to him religiously, and in our imaginations we went along
with him on a magnificent voyage around France. After hear-
ing this story, it was no surprise that we saw Uncle Sulphart so
rarely.

Papa listened as we did, but he asked questions sometimes.
That was the only time in my life that I heard him take an
interest in someone else's life. Sulphart didn't have to be
begged to tell what he had seen, and often it was not so

pleasant. "All over," he said, "people are groaning under the burdens, yet life is precious." Oh, yes! Sulphart saw the misery and he heard the complaints of the workers and peasants, who worked all day for a piece of bread.

"We will have the revolution yet," he said. "We had 1848 for nothing; the Republic is a fraud, like the monarchy and the empire. It can't go on like this. I've seen farms overflowing with riches while the servants were fed from troughs, like pigs, sleeping in straw. Poor devils, their backs were bowed like beasts, from fear of their master." And in the cities he visited, it was even worse. Misery without even country air. Dirty hovels, no right to talk back or you would be chased by dragoons with blows from the flat of a saber. "Sometimes there are people who are so fed up that they stop working. That is a strike—as they say—but it doesn't work either. They have to eat, as little as that may be, so soon they are forced to go back to the factory."

We listened to this with wide eyes. Papa was right when he said there were people worse off than we. When it came down to it, we didn't have too much to complain about, although Uncle seemed to think otherwise. Papa suspected that he was a socialist—a "red"—who wanted to burn everything down. Poor Sulphart! In my eyes, his only "fault" was that he saw so much more than we did and was concerned about it. He left on New Year's Eve, after he had made several sales in our *coron*.

We walked with him to the edge of the village. Zéphyrin plodded resignedly, his head low, pulling the cart up the incline of the road to Cambrai. Gros Loup ran ahead joyously. He soon disappeared from our view; then, in turn, the donkey passed out of sight. "Tonton" Sulphart turned one last time and waved to us, swinging his leather hat. I never saw him again. He and his animals were killed in 1916 in a bombardment near the front, where he was trying to sell his wares. Nothing was left of donkey, wagon, or master.

. .

The beginning of 1908, marked by the departure of our uncle, was also notable because, soon after, my sister Lucie asked me to be the godmother of her son, Alfred, who was to be baptized. My father gave me permission after he consulted Maman. I was old enough, they said, to take on such a big responsibility; at that time, it was real responsibility. God-parents understood that they would have to substitute for the parents if they met with misfortune and raise the godchild. It was worth thinking over. I asked Lucie whom they had chosen for the godfather.

It's tall Auguste, the Santerre boy, she answered. You've met him at our house several times. Well, I refused right away. He didn't please me at all, that boy! I thought him too skinny, too awkward. But mutual acceptance was required among godparents. I don't know what excuse they trotted out for Auguste, who had already been asked, to let him know that it wouldn't work, but, in the end, it was one of my nephews who replaced him.

On the baptismal day, I carried little Alfred in my arms to the church, where the bells were ringing. The priest quickly did his job, for he knew that his parishioners had no time to lose in ritual. He didn't officiate in fancy ceremonies very often, except for the people from the château. My sister gave the priest five sous and then we went back to her house. I didn't give the baby a present. That was perfectly understand-able; no one was surprised. It was obvious that no one my age had sous to spare. My parents never gave me any money, because they couldn't. We quickly drank cups of chicory and I went back to the house, where my father and my sisters hadn't stopped weaving.

For several weeks, when I brought the cloth to Haguet, the merchant's agent, who lived three houses down the *coron*, I had been invited to stay for soup. I didn't like their soup that much, it was too thick. But at the table I was seated near

Louis, the oldest son, a nice little curly-headed blond. He was very attentive toward me. He passed me pieces of bread and poured me water with a smile. I was touched by these attentions, which didn't escape the eyes of Mr. Haguet, a big, jovial, and sly man. He thought I was good enough and he was content to see his son's interest in me.

These dinners, repeated almost every week, made my parents curious. When they questioned me, I explained freely. I admitted that the Haguet boy was very nice and that those dinners were pleasant. Bravely, I went so far as to say that I found him handsome and he pleased me. I got no further. For the first time in my life, I saw my father angry, with a terrible rage that swept over everything in its path. He rose, his face all blue. I was bluntly told, in one breath, that I was shameless and insolent, and had no respect for my parents. As I've said, my father never struck me, but that day I thought he would.

I had dared to praise a boy without his permission! That was an enormous crime, an unbelievable blunder, beyond my poor father's comprehension. My mother never flinched. She bowed her head and let the storm pass. Besides, it didn't last long. As quickly as it had come, it ended. When he sat down again, my father asked my mother's pardon for getting carried away. "Today the young will do anything," he said, by way of excuse. Then, turning toward me, stroking his beard, he added: "You will not go back to Haguet's to deliver our work. Their exploitation of others disturbs me. I know that if it's not them, it's someone else, but still!"

He paused, falling silent for a moment, and then added his judgment of my "crush." "The Haguet boy, like his father, doesn't have a good head. Furthermore, he is frail and small. Men who aren't strong don't father good children." I was irritated by his opinion, which seemed exaggerated, but of course I said nothing. Papa finally finished his scolding. Never in my life have I heard him say so much at one time.

"Listen well, 'our' Marie" (I was called Marie to distinguish me from my mother, who had the same first name), "you are still too young to marry. You have to wait at least two years. Before that, nothing doing! I have decided."

"Our" Marie, "our" Edwige; when he used the plural possessive, it was understood that he was speaking for himself and our mother too. Although she never said what she thought, it was natural that she would feel the same as he. Also, the "I have decided" meant that it was useless to try again. It was really unnecessary for him to say that it would never happen again. Nevertheless, my father used this expression to impress me with his authority. The next Saturday evening, I didn't eat at the Haguets'. I never ate there again, and it was Emérance who took the bolts of woven cloth. Before mass on Sunday, my father went to see the agent. I don't know what they discussed, but no one ever talked of my puppy love again. At least, not of that one.

I thought back on my "adventure" with the Haguets. Maybe Papa was right to say that the son was sickly. Still, he looked handsome to me. Sure he was short, but so what? I wasn't so tall myself. Wouldn't I bear healthy children anyway? And his mustache, blond and fine, in a period when most men wore beards, seemed to be the ultimate in refinement. I imagined that a man with a mustache like that would have tender feelings for a woman and wouldn't be crude like the others. The Haguet son would never harvest sugar beets. I sensed it; I divined it. But maybe, after all, I was wrong? Papa was surely right as usual. Since he had said it, the boy was not for me. Come on, forget these dreams, these forbidden thoughts. It was better to trust my father, who had more experience than me because he was married.

For the time being, I gave no thought to marriage. In my head it seemed a distant and unlikely event. I was so little, so thin. Who would want me?

In April that same year, definitely a month full of happen-

41

ings, Maman gave my sisters and me some amazing news. While my father had gone to the coal mines for fuel—he went for the day—she gathered the three of us together and her words had the effect of a bomb. "We are not going to the country next month. Your father and I are really worn out, so we will weave all year around. The priest wrote to the Saint-Martin farm in our name. We'll see next year."

My sisters and I were struck dumb. This complete upset in our lives seemed impossible. It made us uneasy. Too many traditions were being overturned. And those interminable days in the cellar, all summer long, already seemed beyond enduring. Still, we said nothing. Maman understood what we were feeling. She was also surely concerned about our suffering from weaving without the break, such as it was, of going to the country. It was two years before I again went to the Seine-Inférieure; by then I was married. My parents never returned.

In the evening, when my father came in to dinner, I looked at him while we ate our soup in silence. Alerted by what Maman had told us, I examined him carefully and I noticed how old he looked. His beard was gray. I had never noticed that before. I was ashamed that it had taken my mother's explanation for me to see this. How is it possible to live with loved ones without noticing these profound changes? As I ate my soup, I looked closely at my mother and saw, to my surprise, the same aging. Her hair, sticking out from under her piped bonnet, was gray, like my father's, and there were deep wrinkles in her cheeks. Both of them were also less surefooted. It was incredible! They were old! Later, at my loom, I painfully figured it out: Papa was seventy and Maman was sixty-one![1]

That evening, we whispered in our loft—where, incidentally, my sisters and I were beginning to feel cramped. I told them what I had figured out. They couldn't understand; but did we ever understand each other? We spoke so little to each other. There was no time for words in our life. Our goals were simple: to eat, to sleep, and to work.

The next morning, our legs moved the looms' pedals more quickly. The next Saturday, it turned out that our production had increased somewhat. That increase continued over the weeks. And the dreaded summer passed more easily than we had hoped it would. In fact, to make ends meet, Maman had to skip meat completely, and we didn't get a snack in the afternoons. We mended our clothes more, and our clogs were "resoled" with old leather straps from the harnesses of our looms.

Since we missed the fresh air of the country, we had to replace it somehow. Each day, we went outside after lunch for a slightly longer break. The girls who spent the summer in the *coron* met on the embankment that surrounded the village and overhung the road. We sat on the grass in a group. Our youth made us attractive despite our shabby dress. We giggled at little jokes, so innocent that I've long since forgotten them. What did we talk about? About our work, the number of handkerchiefs woven the day before.

Some girls went to dances every once in a while, and they told us about their evenings. My sisters and I never went, but I, at least, never regretted it. What would I do, exhausted as I was and not knowing how to dance? Sometimes our girlfriends found lovers while dancing a polka. We knew some who got engaged and married that way. I never thought about marriage after the scene with my father. In fact, I had barely thought of it before he scolded me about it. It was only after his outburst that I secretly had the notion that the Haguet boy wanted to marry me.

While the girls gossiped on the bank, their mothers also walked around. But they practically ran, pour souls, because there was always work to do at home. The men who were too old to leave the *coron*, like my father, sat on their doorsteps and smoked their pipes, speaking from house to house in the short phrases of men not used to idle conversation.

Once winter came, there was an added attraction. The boys, back from the country, would walk along the road in groups by age. They weren't that elegant, dressed in hand-me-downs from their fathers and clogs that they stuffed with straw in the winter. That didn't prevent them from boasting. They signaled to us and called at us, emboldened by their number. We responded with prudent "*bonjours*," because our mothers were nearby and, though they walked rapidly, they were paying close attention to what was going on.

In this noisy group, I noticed a boy who was tall, as long as a day without bread. He was very thin and moved awkwardly in a shirt with too-short sleeves and trousers that ended above his ankles. I recognized him; it was Auguste, the Santerre boy, the one that I didn't like and hadn't wanted to be the godfather at Alfred's baptism. Suddenly I was ashamed of having rejected him, poor devil. He had never done anything to me. Because it seemed that he was looking at me, I smiled at him to make up for my wickedness. In the clear March sun, I saw his eyes for the first time. He had noticed my smile and responded to it.

His eyes, my God! They were so beautiful, so blue, so good. Ah, Auguste, my kind, my tender Auguste, it was that day, before you left several weeks later for the country, it was then that I fell in love with you, like that, blindly, in one instant!

Ah, my Pépé, that day I should have tumbled down the bank at a run and curled up with you, felt your long arms around me, as we often did later in our life together. But I didn't know! How much time we lost, all on account of appearances. We could have had many extra hours together during those two years! Oh, yes, my Pépé, I should have, I should have, I should have. . . . Now that you aren't here, so many years later, my God, I regret that I didn't ignore Papa and Maman, that I didn't go to you, so sad, so alone, so lost, right away. To you who waited for me, who longed for me. My poor, dear Pépé, I can't turn back the clock, but I weep over what we might have done.

How I loved you, my big one, right away, in my heart and in my head. The rest, you taught me later. But that was never important. What counted our whole life long together was all of you, with your gentleness, your never-ending goodness. My God, if all women could have a husband like I had—an ignoramus, according to people who went to school, because he knew neither how to read nor how to write—but so tender, so attentive to his "Marie-Cat." How I miss him now.

So it went. Every day of the week, at the beginning of the afternoon, Auguste and his friends would walk down the road and we smiled at each other. Toward the end of April, while looking at me from afar with his clear eyes, he gathered the courage to yell to me: "I'm leaving tomorrow. Goodbye! We'll see each other again on Saint Catherine's Day."

I can't tell you how much sorrow I felt those summer months in the half-deserted *coron*. He was gone, and only children walked along the road. My sisters and I, and our few remaining friends, still went to the sun-warmed embankment. It was more out of duty, to preserve our health, than out of need, especially for me, so miserable with my new secret which I dared not share with anyone, paralyzed by the emotion called love. It was awful.

The months passed, from bed to cellar, table to embankment. And handkerchiefs piled on handkerchiefs. Each week, I saved a little more thread for the cloth in my trousseau. I knew that if I were to marry, it would be to him, and the bits of cloth piled up in my thread box.

Tomorrow was my saint's day: Saint Catherine's. November had cast a glaze of ice over the court that made the red brick houses seem to shiver and huddle together. Smoke puffed from the chimneys as though the troubles and cares of those inside the houses were being expelled in the thin and smelly wisps. The water no longer flowed freely at the fountain, and the ice in the trough had to be broken into pieces and melted on the sturdy little Flemish stove.

At 4:00 A.M., before sunrise, the lamps began to flicker in the cellar windows. And the rattling back and forth of the shuttles across the looms began. The people who had gone to the country had returned yesterday, their faces tanned by the harvest sun and by the cold and humid wind of the sugar-beet country.

Among the houses in which weaving started up again was the one where Auguste lived with his parents and his eight brothers and sisters.[2] I tried to find out about his family after dinner, very carefully, because of my earlier experience. Maman, it seemed, didn't suspect anything. Maybe she thought that I was curious because of my refusal to have Auguste near me as the godfather at Alfred's baptism. She dropped some details: "Those Santerres are in a bad way. The father is unsociable and brutal, and the mother lives in fear of her husband. The oldest of the nine children is Auguste—you know, Marie, the one that you refused!—a strong, good boy, I hear, and one of the best weavers in the *coron*. He's back from the country. I saw him this morning when I went to buy bread."

All this interested me very much, but I looked as unconcerned as I could. However, I jumped when my mother said that she had met Auguste. As soon as we had finished our lunch soup, I did the dishes quickly. Then, right away, I ran—what am I saying?—I flew to the embankment.

I was cold as death. There wasn't a soul outdoors. I took a deep breath. Would he come? I didn't have long to worry. I heard the sound of his sabots clattering as he strode along; then I saw him coming, awkward as ever, with his shrunken shirt and trousers, his sabots insulated with straw. It was him at last! All summer I had dreamed of him. He came close, pretending to look elsewhere. I in turn pretended that I didn't see him. But that couldn't last. The sound of his clogs came closer and closer on the macadam road. Was it the cold that made both our faces red? I realized later that it wasn't that at all. It was the emotion of seeing each other, without a soul around, as chance would have it.

"Oh! Marie-Catherine, what a nice surprise! How do you do?"

"Auguste, of all people! Back already? How did your work go?"

We were both so silly! He stopped and backed away, looking shabbier than ever in his old clothes. But what I saw were his blue eyes, clear as spring water. And what did he see in me? I was ashamed of my long, gray cotton skirt and my woolen hood.

"You look much bigger and stronger, Marie-Catherine."

Then panic struck me. If Papa surprised him paying me such compliments, I would get a licking. That was enough for this time. I turned away in haste. But (the height of shamelessness!) I dared call back to him, "Goodbye, Auguste, see you tomorrow!"

That afternoon, my shuttle stopped frequently and then started again rapidly. Troubled by this irregular rhythm, my father asked about my health. Maman, who was upstairs winding bobbins for our shuttles, came down to find out why I was doing such choppy work.

Auguste and I met this way almost every day, under the gray sky, a sky that finally belched thick snow on Christmas Day. We met at the embankment, where we were often alone together. Little by little, we conversed more calmly, though always at a distance of ten meters. I learned a lot about him, and he came to know more about me; we spoke simply, with no lost words. When I went back home, no one seemed to be surprised that I had braved the cold long after my sisters had given up going out.

At Christmas, Papa decided to kill the rabbit that he had

been fattening in the cellar. We hardly ever saw meat any-more, and he didn't want the rabbit to get stolen before we had a chance to eat it. While we were at mass, he simmered the poor rabbit and some potatoes over the fire. My sister Lucie and her husband were invited to this feast. After the meal, there was nothing left of the rabbit except the large bones. The beast, cartilage and all, had been devoured in appreciative silence. For dessert, we had a pot of boiled chest-nuts that my brother-in-law had gathered in the forests. Those wild chestnuts were sweet and delicious. To make the most of them, we didn't shell them. We ate them by biting them between our teeth and sucking the husks for a long time. Last came the bowls of boiling chicory.

As we sat in satisfied bliss, Lucie dropped a bombshell, all the louder because it was unexpected. "You know, Papa," she said, "after Monday, the Santerre boy will be living at our home." Sitting across from her, I choked on my "coffee." Lucie continued her explanation, unaware—I thought—of the confusion she was causing in my mind. "Auguste," she said, "doesn't want to live at home anymore. It's hell with his father. He hasn't a sou to his name. His father takes all the money he makes. So he has asked me if he could lodge with us, paying room and board. Paul thought we should; it will help us make ends meet."

Father approved of this arrangement. "I like that boy a lot, he's a strong fellow. He'll make his way, but he had bad luck with his parents." Lucie continued, "Auguste will tell his father this evening. But he's afraid of what will happen if they are alone together when he breaks the news."

That things hadn't gone well was the first thing I found out the next day. When Auguste arrived at our rendezvous, his face was covered with bruises and he had a black eye. He told me that he had been given a monumental beating, with blows from sabots, fists, and a belt. I was horrified. "But you have to fight back, defend yourself!" I yelled at him from the top of the embankment. I can still hear his quiet response, his simple explanation: "But, Marie-Catherine, one doesn't fight back against one's father." I was indignant. I wanted Auguste to come to me so that I could bathe his bruises, his eyes. Alas, he went off, limping slightly. God, he was in awful shape!

Throwing caution to the wind, I exploded angrily when I got home. I could talk about Auguste because Lucie had brought up his problems already. My father, who was at his loom in the cellar, listened to my tale. Maman came down too, and she shook her head with pity as she said, "Old Santerre is going too far, whipping his son that way!" Without halting the to-and-fro of his shuttle, Papa agreed. He hated beatings, probably because he himself had been beaten so often.

I murmured to myself as I went back to work. Was I imagining it? It seemed to me that, as I sat down, my parents exchanged quick and tender smiles, as they did when they shared a personal thought.

So, along with our meetings at the embankment, I waited anxiously for visits from Lucie. She seldom came because she didn't have much time, poor thing. I wanted to know how things were working out with Auguste. I was looking for an excuse to visit my sister since she never came to the house, but I couldn't find any. Papa—whether it was on purpose, I don't know, and it doesn't matter—Papa helped me out. "It's been a long time," he said, "since you've seen Alfred, your godson. Go to your sister's house this evening and see how he is doing. But come back early."

I was overwhelmed at the suggestion. Come dinnertime, I ran to Lucie's and, as expected, I met Auguste. For the first time, I sat at the same table as him, drinking a cup of chicory. He told me that there was open war now between his father and him. What bothered him most, besides never seeing his mother, whom he adored, was that his father had refused to let him take his loom when he left home. Luckily, my brother-in-law Paul was able to loan him one.

"I'm going to work at this loom until my departure for the country, Marie-Catherine. I will be able to put a few sous aside," he whispered. His voice was barely audible. He was as red as a glowing briquette in the Flemish stove when he added, "I would like to find a tender and courageous wife to marry, and to have a house of my own." He managed to say all this only with enormous effort. Once the words were out, he jumped up, jostling the bench, and unceremoniously rushed down the trap door to the cellar. There he rejoined Paul, whose loom could be heard moving up and down regularly.

Lucie, who was winding bobbins in a corner of the room, turned to me smiling. She remarked, as if to excuse Auguste for what he had said, "If you only knew how miserable he is!" She spoke—did she realize it?—to someone who was already converted.

Auguste wanted to marry. But whom? I thought he didn't know anyone except me, but on reflecting, I couldn't be sure. Maybe he had a good friend I didn't know about. I was consumed with fierce jealousy at the thought, and I went back home feeling desperate.

Before I went to sleep, I told my parents about Auguste's situation and plans. Bit by bit, he had found a place in our family, and it seemed natural for me to speak of him as of a brother. Maman approved of his plan to marry. "Surely," she said firmly, "it's the best thing for the poor fellow to do."

Then my father, who was checking the edge of a long piece of finished cloth, turned slowly. In his gnarled hands, the creamy linen unrolled rapidly, as he felt along the length in search of any faults. In the flickering light of the kerosene lamp I felt his eyes seeking mine out. He said, and I've never in all my life forgotten it: "It's a woman like you that he needs, Marie. He's been so unlucky, that fellow. So, if he pleases you, marry him."

Chapter Four

"M arie-Catherine Gardez, do you take this man, Auguste Santerre, as your lawfully wedded husband?" My "I do" was barely audible.

"Auguste Santerre, do you take this woman, Marie-Catherine Gardez, as your lawfully wedded wife?" His "I do" was more firm, but my fiancé was as white as chalk.

It was December 13, 1909, just ten days before my eighteenth birthday.[1] I was marrying the man whom I loved and who loved me. One never forgets such a day. It was a mild winter, so mild that they hadn't even lit a fire in the small room of the Avesnes town hall. On the darkened pine table in front of us, there was a small, newly filled-in document, our marriage license. Above the mayor, Mr. Belloy, a tall clock, called an oxeye because of the design on its face, marked the silence following our "I do's" with its noisy ticktock. The first seconds of my life as a wife are inscribed in my memory this way: tick tock, tick tock.

The mayor was regaining his good spirits and cheery way. Both had been rudely tried that morning. We had waited an hour and a half for Auguste's parents, whose consent was necessary because he was still a minor. We'd spent that hour and a half peering out of the dusty panes of the town-hall window, looking for the Santerres. The marriage was scheduled for 10:00 A.M. Paul and Lucie, my witnesses, were there, stiff in their Sunday clothes. Papa and Maman, huddled on the bench, looked old but happy as they waited patiently. And the oxeye clock marked the increasingly uneasy wait with its ticktock.

A very old and very dirty man sat in the corner of the room, scribbling endlessly. The scratch of his straight pen marked the passage of time. We watched respectfully as the metal beak moved across the register. Papa and Auguste were especially impressed by his silent work. I recognized the man in the corner—it was the public schoolmaster, who worked as the mayor's secretary. In the village, they said he was very wise. Seeing him write so quickly and surely, we had no trouble believing it.

At 11:00, Mr. Belloy came back to see if we were finally ready. His frock coat was buttoned over his paunch, and a tricolored sash was fastened sloppily around his waist. The mayor was irritated, and he would have kicked us out long before if he hadn't respected my father so much. He angrily called the village crier—it was still old François—and ordered him to go get "that double-damned old Santerre who is always acting contrary to everyone else."

Who knows what diplomacy and persuasion old François employed to succeed in his mission? The clock read almost 11:30 by the time Auguste's parents came, his father in fury and his mother, resigned, following behind him. To rub in their point that they had been forced to come, they wore what they had on when they were "pulled away" from their work. He was wearing a long gray smock, she a faded black dress and sabots on her feet. Mr. Belloy was relieved to see them come. He didn't like family discord; it disrupted the harmony of the village.

But after reading the wedding ceremony, he gave in to his hard feelings, congratulating—contrary to custom—only my parents, "good people who honor the town with their honesty." And he gave us, with his compliments, our marriage license, which we kept with us for the rest of our lives.

Not a word was exchanged among those present. Auguste and I left the town hall, each contributing a sou for the poor of the commune. The schoolmaster hadn't once deigned to raise his head. We were mere "clericals," unworthy of the least notice. He crossly continued to fill the pages of the big register with his quick writing.

We went to the church in silence. Paul, the only one who didn't seem to be concerned about things, observed that it was quite mild for the month of December. Papa groaned. It was just the sort of comment he despised. Mr. Santerre said nothing. His face was closed, hard, forbidding. The priest hadn't come yet. Someone had warned him that we would be late. Pushing open the door, we entered the dilapidated little church, which, in contrast to the outdoors, was freezing cold.

Auguste and I kneeled in front of the altar together while the others sat down, rattling the chairs, which echoed mournfully over the flagstones. There was a smell of mildew in the cold church which kept me from concentrating on my prayers. It was a pity, but it was there and I couldn't do anything about it. The strong smell obsessed me, so I thought of the incense used in Sunday mass. I would have liked to have had incense. It seemed to me that incense would have made the ceremony more serious, more moving. As for music, there wasn't a chance. The grocer's daughter, who played piano, charged three francs to play the harmonium for marriages and burials. Of course we didn't have a penny for such an extravagance!

Finally the priest made a hasty entry, pulling his surplice over his head. He fastened it while genuflecting rapidly before the altar, stepping up lightly because a step had collapsed. The altar boy walked in front of him, carrying a big leather-bound book with bent corners. Then came the blessing of our marriage. In a voice that was strong despite his age, the priest spoke Latin words which we didn't understand, and the altar boy mumbled replies.

Between two responses, the priest abruptly questioned us, hardly opening his mouth to speak: "Do you have the rings?" Auguste, surprised by this unexpected question, was struck dumb. Then, absentmindedly, he searched in his pocket and nodded his head. He had found the matchbox in which we had placed "our" wedding rings.

When I say "our" wedding rings, I exaggerate. We couldn't afford any. I had Maman's, very delicate, very light, very worn, and Paul had lent his—a silver band—to Auguste. It wasn't until fifteen years later that I received my own, a Christmas gift from my husband. He never had one. Each time he decided to get a ring, we had some disaster that meant he couldn't buy it.

"It's not important, Marie-Cat," he would say. "What counts is that we are happy." Still, I held on to my wedding ring. Today it is as delicate as Maman's was when I got married.

We walked out of the church together after the ceremony. We had placed two sous in the collection plate. It cost us six sous in all, and that was something, because we were poor. But we had to do it. It would have been dishonorable not to celebrate a marriage. Paul gave a sou to the altar boy. Excited by the unexpected tip, the kid caught hold of the thick bell rope hanging by the door. He swung on it and offered us a princely bell-ringing that created a stir in the whole village.

People asked, "What important marriage is being celebrated?" It was ours and it wasn't important, but was it beautiful! I squeezed my husband's arm tightly, and he straightened up proudly. How handsome he was, my Auguste, all dressed in black! He had made an incredibly good deal: the wife of the baker, Arsène, had sold him her husband's marriage suit for seven francs, on credit until November. "My man could never squeeze into it with the paunch he has now," she said laughing. "So take advantage of it." No matter how hard I tried, I couldn't imagine Arsène ever fitting into that suit. To be sure, it was a little big for Auguste, but still! How people change over the years!

I wore my Sunday dress, but Maman had sewed on a little ruffle of white lace which she had salvaged from a blouse she no longer wore. That blouse was very pretty, and I wondered how she could have afforded it. On my head, she tied my first-communion veil into a sort of pouf. Then she lovingly arranged my long blond hair, which she had washed carefully with camomile the day before.

The only hitch was that we couldn't buy or borrow any decent shoes. We didn't have so much as a down payment for them. So Papa used his ingenuity. He blackened both of our clogs with the soot from the little stove. Then when that had dried, he waxed the wood with a rind of salt pork. It was a real success; you would have thought we were wearing patent-leather shoes.

Our little marriage procession returned to the house. At the cobbled path that led to Bertrand's grocery store, the Santerres turned without a word to go to their home. A second before this separation, father and son looked quickly at each other—and that was it. My heart was heavy to see them turn away like that, his parents, arms swinging, his mother following his father with her head down. My joy—so great, so profound—was partly spoiled. All my life, I've grudged them their behavior that day.

We were back at our cottage. Because of the temperature—it was warm, unseasonably warm—we had left the door open. My sisters were waiting for us. They had been working: "A marriage in the family is no excuse to take off from everything," my father said.

Still, he had decided to celebrate the marriage that he had

approved and encouraged. He had gone to the brewery in the morning to buy a pitcher of beer. By buying in quantity, he got it for twenty sous less.

Maman put on her smock over her familiar black best dress, decorated with the pearls she always wore to Sunday mass. She went solemnly to the gray cupboard by the window, where it was cool. She took out a package wrapped in greasy paper, which she carried gravely to the table. Before our astonished eyes, she unwrapped eight lamb chops. Paul and Lucie were going to eat with us.

How had my poor mother managed to put this meat on the table? By what miracles of saving had she scraped together the money for this extravagant purchase? Paul made a joke, but in the process he caused bad feelings. He said mockingly that Maman must have taken advantage of an epidemic of hoof-and-mouth disease among the sheep to make a good buy. My father didn't appreciate this smart remark. He scolded Paul severely for his bad joke. Meat was holy. One didn't joke about it! Just because one doesn't eat it often doesn't make it right to suggest that someone is serving diseased meat at lunch. Paul, admitting that he had gone too far, humbly asked pardon.

While my sisters set the table in a clatter of plates, Auguste and I stood silently hand in hand in the doorway, immersed in our happiness. I was suddenly struck by an unbelievable thought. This man whom I loved, who was to be my husband from then on, this man with whom I would sleep that evening—I had never kissed him! Profiting from my surprise and our solitude on the doorstep, without thinking, I raised myself on his neck—my God, he was tall!—and my lips touched his cheek. He was stupefied and annoyed because of my parents behind us. But he must have liked it because he seized me in turn. Turning, he found my mouth and gave it a long kiss. It was my turn to be ashamed, but I also found it awfully nice. That was our first kiss.

Paul, who had gone out, coughed quietly to announce his return discreetly, thus ending our blissful embrace. Then, maybe to hide his embarassment and to excuse himself, he mischievously hummed his favorite tune, which I knew well:

If you think I will tell you
Whom I dare to admire,
Well, I wouldn't tell you
For a whole empire. . . .

Auguste and I remembered this "Chanson de Fortunio"—I didn't learn its name until later, when I heard it on the radio—one evening in 1918, while mourning poor Paul, killed in the war at the front at Fère-en-Tardenois.

The wedding day was pure joy! Each place on the table was marked by a little cream-colored linen napkin, secretly woven by my father. Next to the thick round loaf of bread, there was a little onion *flamique,* a present from Arsène, the baker, moved perhaps by the thought of Auguste in his old formal suit. The chops bubbled in their juice on the little stove, which cracked joyously, as if to participate in the celebration. In the round oven of the stove, the potatoes, which had been peeled and rubbed with garlic, puffed up properly without popping.

We all stood by the table. Auguste was at my side. Papa made a rapid sign of the cross and said: "Lord bless the meal that we are about to eat here. Praise to You, our God. Today, we ask You to make Marie-Catherine and Auguste happy and good spouses. Amen."

God heard my father. Happy and good spouses we were; nothing, for one minute, even one second, ever separated us, except death, from which there is no escape; it takes us all in the end, rich and poor. That is the ultimate justice, and that's why I believe in God. Happiness can be found everywhere, whether people sleep between silk sheets or on straw. What counts is joy in your heart, in your head, even if you don't have a bank account. And deep down, no matter who we are, when it comes down to it, we will all die. And we are all buried in the same earth. Auguste said that that was equality, and he was right. Now people say otherwise; I prefer that simple way of saying it.

After dinner, we got ready for our first night together. We were going to sleep in my parents' house. The bed, the cupboard, and the table we had ordered, as was the tradition, from the village cabinetmaker were not quite ready. We were lucky enough to have found a little cottage next to my parents'. We moved in two days later, as soon as we got our furniture. On our wedding night, my sisters slept at Paul's house, and we slept in their place in the loft.

People make a big deal out of the wedding night. I don't see why. Although it was very difficult for her to explain, Maman had warned me of what awaited me that evening. She spoke with great care, choosing her words so as not to scare me. She was wrong to worry so much. I wasn't afraid and didn't expect anything out of the ordinary. I already loved Auguste as he was. Any "extras" to come would just add to my pleasure.

Besides, the "extras" didn't come right away. That evening, we settled into our little garret. Poor Auguste was so tall that he had a hard time taking off his clothes. His long arms banged against the boards of the roof. I was used to the space so I had already put on the new cotton nightgown printed with big roses that Maman secretly gave me. I waited calmly and finally felt Auguste, in a nightshirt, slide to my side. We were very cramped and could barely move. My husband took me in his arms and kissed me. But we could hear Papa tossing and coughing below us. So my husband spoke in my ear, softly so that no one else would hear. "Let's sleep, Marie-Cat." (That was the first time he called me by this pet name.) "Let's sleep. It's hard to say, but it wouldn't be good with your parents just below." I understood. I fell asleep tranquilly.

That was my wedding night. The real one was two days later, in our own house. We waited until then—after all, we had our whole lives ahead of us to make of what we wished. We weren't put off by several hours.

The next day, we began working with my parents. Paul loaned Auguste a loom that we set up as well as we could in the cellar, which was already crowded with looms. Auguste was a very able worker, at least as good as Papa, and he got right to work. Maman had decided to work even longer and wind his bobbins too, which saved him precious time. Ah! Those first hours together, how beautiful they were! The shuttles went to and fro. Papa, happy to have us near him, was pleased to sing, and one piece of cloth followed another: the big ones of fine linen that Auguste wove and my much-narrower handkerchiefs. Each week I was able to put a couple of sous aside. They went to the cabinetmaker, whom we had promised to pay off in two years.

We continued living the same way as my parents. For food, soup and chicory, Auguste went to see Arsène about getting an accounting stick, which was given him with no questions. We also had an account at the grocer's. My father's reputation served us well. Three times a day, we went home to eat or to drink a bowl of chicory. I was proud and happy in my cottage. It was much smaller than my parents' and it didn't have a cellar: that was why we had to weave at their house. But our three pieces of furniture and the little stove we had bought secondhand from a neighbor were enough for us. I polished and repolished everything. I had to scrub the tiles of the floor because they were all stained. It was hard work, but I got them clean.

The floor shone after that, and the two handfuls of sawdust I scattered after each washing protected the tiles. My father had to teach Auguste how to make his own fuel bricks. He chose a Sunday afternoon. Then, by the stove, there were thirty bricks drying; the funny odor that I had smelled all my childhood in my parents' house came with them. Everything was so familiar that I was never homesick in my new cottage. It had the same atmosphere as my parents'. At first, we had only one pair of sheets, a present from Maman; well worn, but sheets nonetheless. When I washed them, we slept right on the straw mattress. I couldn't buy a second pair of sheets until eight months later, after we went to the country.

We left in May, as usual. Auguste went to see the priest, who wrote a letter for us to the company. He told the agent about our marriage and explained that we wanted to work as our parents had. An answer came three weeks later. I painfully deciphered it, after having opened the big gray envelope addressed to "Mr. and Mrs. Auguste Santerre" with trembling hands. The agent congratulated us on our marriage and said that he was pleased to accept our offer—he was certain we would be very good workers. In the letter there was also a big sheet of blue paper covered with signatures and stamps. It was a money order for twelve francs.

My husband explained that it was probably the price of our transportation, which the company, considering us reliable, had sent us. Twelve francs! I had been anxious about paying our railroad fare, but now I was wild with joy. I wanted to go get the money right away, but Auguste refused. He put the money order in our family strongbox and said that we would get the money when we needed it. "That way we won't be tempted to spend it."

As the months passed until time to go to the country, we were happy, very happy. We continued working on the same schedule—from 4:00 A.M. to 10:00 P.M.—and I didn't complain, despite my additional duties as housewife. I wasn't tired. As for my husband, he met every hardship head on, despite his skinniness. He didn't talk much, like my father, but that never bothered me. Neither of them could read either, but they never felt any loss. I tried vainly to teach

Auguste what little I knew. He never wanted to learn. It's enough, he would say, to have one scholar in the family.

The one thing that he always gave me, and never stopped giving me, was tenderness. While we were working at our looms, he would turn to me ten times a day, worried. "You aren't tired, are you?" And at the table, he kept an eye on what I ate. It had to be as much as he got. We worked equally hard. Therefore we had to eat equally. He never changed his mind. Even if I laughingly refused to eat more sometimes, unable to swallow another spoonful of soup, he didn't let me get away with it.

At noon, after lunch, we went hand in hand to get some fresh air on "our" embankment. We passed my girlfriends, who were jealous of me. I was now "Auguste's wife" and people said that I was very lucky. We would stroll around in the sun there. Sometimes, to amuse ourselves, we played a little game. Auguste would back down to the road and we would talk at a distance, as if we weren't married.

"So, Marie-Catherine, how's it going with you?"

"Fine, Monsieur Auguste. And your work?"

And we would go on like that, one after the other, chatting. But my husband couldn't keep up this game for long. He would climb up the embankment at a run. And those days it wasn't unusual for us to return home suddenly, locking our door carefully behind us. And then we would be late getting back to work. My legs felt like cotton batting at times like those.

And Papa, half-grumbling, half-smiling in his now white beard, sighed. "Ah! My God, youth! Work never gets done quickly when you're young. It's true that we were young once, but it's hard to remember it."

At the end of April, we packed our baggage for our departure to the country. I was happy to go back to the Saint-Martin farm, but at the same time I felt a twinge in my heart. For the first time, I would leave my father and mother behind, for they no longer went to the country. They were too worn out. The cottage was emptying out, with me gone and Emérance soon to marry the young "mail" driver and move with him to Cambrai. The next year, Anatolie married one of Paul's friends and went to live near Paris. My poor old parents were finally alone.

When we arrived at the farm that year, we, too, had a little room of our own. We were comfortable because we didn't have any children. Not then. We didn't want any yet, and Auguste was a lad with self-discipline. My brother-in-law Paul had explained to him at length how one could have kids only when one wanted them. And Auguste followed his advice scrupulously.

As the months passed, we did our daily tasks together. Our work was set by nature's rhythm, following the seasons. Thinning, hoeing, spreading fertilizer, reaping, clearing the fields. The sun and the rain were our daily companions: we had to live with their whims. Bent to the earth, we served her, as we would for the rest of our lives. She was definitely a hard and demanding mistress, but she fed us, when it came down to it. Auguste said that, in cities, people actually died of starvation. At least we always had soup and fresh air around us. That's why we wouldn't have wanted to work in a factory if we'd had the chance. There, one couldn't even be sure of eating every day.

At the Saint-Martin farm, we quickly earned the reputation of being hard-working and conscientious. Our earnings mounted as we worked. Auguste was first-rate at hoeing. I could never keep up with him, so he would come back and help me when he had finished his plot. The rows added to rows, the sheaves to sheaves. The agent was pleased. We were thrilled to see, when we collected our pile of silver, the day before Saint Catherine's Day, that he had given us a bonus. I had never seen such a thing and thought it was an error. I asked him about it and he replied, "No, it isn't an error, Madame Santerre. Both of you work hard. It's only fair to reward hard work."

When we returned home in November, Auguste's big leather purse was well filled. We could pay off the cabinet-maker early, and he gave us a big discount besides. I was pleased, because we were going to need money. I was expecting a child.

It was in July, during the harvest, that we both had the idea of having a child. We already knew that it would be a good season. One evening, at bedtime, Auguste and I talked about it. We said maybe, taking everything into account, it would be better for us to have a child right away, while we were still young. Then, when my husband was forty, the little boy—or girl—would be twenty. I thought that sounded good. It had always bothered me to see my parents so aged when I was still an adolescent. We wouldn't have that problem with our child.

That's why I couldn't go back to the country until 1914. On the other hand, my husband went each season, while I stayed and wove at my parents' house, tending our baby.

He was born April 6, 1911. I was twenty, but I remember it as if it were yesterday. The day before, I had begun to do the laundry—mine and my parents'. I did it in the big cast-iron tub that served the whole *coron*. There were iris bulbs that had been dug up from the nearby fields in the water for bluing. Suddenly I felt pains, and my mother began to worry right away. "Leave the laundry, I'll rinse it," she told me.

But I wouldn't pay attention, and I finally sat down only around 11:00 in the evening. Auguste was furious and, when my pains didn't cease, he put me to bed. Someone called Fat Zulma. It was still she, seeming immortal, who was the village midwife. She glanced at me and her experience stood her in good stead. "I'll return tomorrow morning, she'll do fine," she said.

Auguste lay down on a straw mattress on the floor at the

foot of the bed. He slept with one eye open, jumping up at the least noise. The next morning at dawn, he eagerly set to work cleaning the cottage. Zulma arrived early, but the house was already spotless. The hundred-sou "barrow wheel" and three one-franc pieces were sitting on the table, and the room smelled of delicious real coffee. Auguste knew the tradition so he had also gotten the egg, whose sugared yolk he would soon drop into the midwife's coffee cup.

Maman hadn't wanted to come. She was scared of complications and feared that I would suffer. She didn't want to see that and simply asked my husband to call her if she was urgently needed.

I had been squirming with pain for a while when Zulma finally arrived. I believed that, once she was there, all would go smoothly. It was not as easy as I imagined, however, and I suffered a lot before the baby was born. Auguste, at the end of his rope, ran wildly for my parents, expecting disaster because I was screaming like an animal. But when they all rushed back, it was over. Our son had arrived, and Zulma was already washing him carefully, as she would for nine days, before I was allowed to get out of bed.

Everyone clustered around me respectfully. Grandparents and father alike were overwhelmed with joy. When I told them I intended to name the baby Auguste, his father broke down and cried like a kid. There was coffee for everyone, and the egg in Zulma's cup, which she had already started to sip in a satisfied way. She was pleased with the smooth train of events. And she and my mother harkened back to my own birth, on that icy December evening, when the wolves were howling. It had been twenty years since then.

Finally, the two of us were left alone; no, the three of us. I had to get used to it. From then on, there was one more in the house. My husband never regretted having created that little bundle of flesh that was greedily clutching at my breast. The baby cried even while he sucked strongly.

A bit later, I was enjoying the good vegetable soup that Maman had brought when there was a knock on the door. Auguste opened it. I couldn't believe my eyes! It was his parents. Awkward, ill at ease, they didn't know how to explain their visit. Mr. Santerre made a stab at it: "We came because we heard you had a little one. Our feelings were strong, stronger than we were. We're proud . . . we have to see our grandchild." And without waiting, impatient with curiosity, they went to the little box, suspended from the ceiling by four ropes, that my husband had made to serve as a cradle.

And they were enraptured in their turn. The crabbed face of my father-in-law lit up in a smile. In our families, a baby was always welcome and, when it was a son, it was even better. "He sure is a Santerre, he resembles us," he said.

I didn't think that baby looked like anyone. But I didn't say anything and neither did Auguste, who, all in all, was pretty pleased to see his parents. Since there was some coffee left, he offered it to them, letting them understand that the reconciliation should be complete. The parents-in-law fell right into the role of grandparents, just as my parents had. The mother came up to me and slid something wrapped in paper into my hand. "It's a medallion of the Virgin," she said in a whisper. "Let the child wear it, it will bring him happiness."

All the while, father and son chatted calmly, as if they saw each other daily. There was never another mention of their quarrel. "Tomorrow, Auguste, you must come and get your loom. It hasn't been used since you left. But it should be yours and I am giving it to you." It took a big effort on old Santerre's part to make this offer. Once that was said, he fell silent and drank his coffee. I was glad that Auguste had won his parents back again. He hadn't talked about it, but I felt that he was troubled, saddened by the separation.

For nine days, my husband waited on me. He learned how to make soup. He scrubbed on his hands and knees. He had to spend all his nonworking time on housework, poor fellow! I was stuck in bed moping. After a while I wanted to get up, but he wouldn't hear of it.

So I began my work again only a few days before Auguste's departure for the country, which, alas! came too soon. My sadness grew as the day came closer. Although we had lived together for a relatively short time, Auguste had become part of my life, and the days to come without him seemed intolerable, even in anticipation. Still, with the baby, I couldn't go along with him.

At 5:00 in the morning on his departure day, I went with him to the meeting place for the seasonal laborers leaving from Avesnes. It was the beginning of May, and the sun hadn't risen yet. I had bundled his clothes and some slices of bread and white cheese for the trip. His canteen was full of real coffee, a surprise for him, and the coffee was well sugared. I was extravagant because of the special occasion.

Everyone who was going was there, gathered together. For the first time, I wouldn't share their journey. And Auguste, my Auguste, my dear Auguste, crossed the marketplace without me. I had tears in my eyes, and I was glad that he couldn't see them. Close to seven months without him! My God, what would become of me, without feeling his long arms embracing me every evening, and without being able to sleep wedged close to him? Not to hear his tender voice say, early every morning, while gently shaking me, "Come on, come on, Marie-Cat. It's time to get up."

I felt myself swept with panic and, for a minute, I begged him not to go, to stay with me after all. We could manage. Then I was ashamed to have acted like that when he seemed so brave, and I said, "Above all, be careful not to catch cold and not to let yourself get too wet."

My voice trembled, so, to pull myself together, I straightened his jacket and scarf, as I would for a child. He looked lost also, although he tried to be brave, to look strong. He took my hand and I felt him tremble. Eventually, it was time. They were leaving. So we kissed a long, long kiss until, in the first glimmerings of dawn, a crude voice broke in: "Come on, Santerre, are you almost done?"

My loved one left me abruptly, as if he were running away. I followed him the short distance to the embankment, and then I accompanied him with my eyes until he was lost in the thin light of dawn. I felt as though the world were crumbling, as though Auguste were going to die. Seated on "our" grassy embankment, I cried with great sobs, feeling that I would never be able to stop. It was the thought of the other Auguste, my little one, who waited alone at the house, that pulled me back together.

That summer I worked a lot, more than usual, at my loom. My parents tried to make me slow down. I had never brought so many pieces of cloth to the agent, Haguet's successor, at the end of the week. The Haguets had left the year before, and they were replaced by nice people who lived at the out-skirts of the village. Little Auguste slept in the basket that Maman had made for him from a big piece of cloth and willow switches. My little one grew quickly; he was sweet-tempered and never ill. His grandparents watched over him tenderly, so he was never alone by the stove in the big room. One or another of us was always going up to see him. Papa especially, as he grew old, became fanatically cautious.

I received my first letter in June. It was written in a rough hand by some co-worker of Auguste's, and I had a hard time deciphering the words, not quite understanding what they said. But it was clear that my husband was doing well and that he was working like an animal, as I was, so that the money the two of us would have in November would be about the same as we had earned the year before.

I wrote three or four letters a week to Auguste. For the first time in my life, I realized how useful it was to know how to write. And I felt thankful to my parents for allowing me to learn. So in the evening, very late, the little kerosene lamp burned in the main room of our cottage, while I wrote a message to my husband. I used a school notebook bought at the grocer's and a straight pen with a little bottle of ink. I didn't leave out anything about our poor life in Avesnes. But as it wasn't he who read my letters, there were many things I couldn't say. How I needed him at certain times—in bed, or at the loom. How I missed him. It seemed that I was another person, not connected with myself. Luckily, I had little Auguste, who kept me from worrying more. He grew well, solid as a poor man's child, with good strong bones and a robust appetite.

Little Alfred, my godson, who was going on four years old, liked his cousin very much. He came to see Auguste often and brought his parents with him. These evening visits coming after my often exhausted return from my parents' cellar did me good. We talked of my husband, absent as he was from these gatherings, and Paul argued that we should do as he and Lucie did: not go to the country anymore. Paul never had the taste for outdoor labor. But that wouldn't help our finances, which were never that promising. I knew they worse off than we, and it pained me. Paul and Lucie were so nice! So I often invited them to come have supper with me. Those evenings, I made the soup thicker and heartier than usual and that pleased them. I was sure that Auguste would approve this expense of a few extra sous. He was like me: it upset him for others not to have enough.

While Auguste was gone, I began a new custom. Three times a week, right after the midday soup, I went with my baby to see the Santerre grandparents. They waited impatiently for these visits, and, though they could hardly afford to stop weaving, they would spend a couple of minutes kissing the baby and talking to him. There was poverty in their cottage also, as in most of the houses in the *coron*. Oh, not a dirty poverty, as one sees described in books. No, a clean poverty, in a house that was scoured and scrubbed. I, who complained, was rich compared to them.

They had only the two of them to work, and they were old.[2] The grandmother prepared yarn for the shuttles and the grandfather wove. All the children had left, scattered around the region as agricultural laborers, unskilled workers, or wood-cutters. The old folks were alone. I figured it out often: they must have lived on one hundred sous per week. Bread and potatoes. That was it. As Grandfather Santerre no longer had the strength to get his own coal dust, and because, some weeks, he couldn't buy the peat for fuel, they often had only a few sticks to burn for cooking meals.

Nevertheless, in their life of privation, neither one gave up his standards. They were scrupulously clean, and, when I kissed them, I could smell green soap. But there often wasn't a crumb of bread in the cupboard or on the table. One day, I took them a little package of chicory. I had noticed that they drank nothing but linden tea, straight, with no sugar. The grandfather went to get the linden from the big trees that flanked the entrance to the château and then dried it.

I never heard them complain. Not a word, not a regret. Hours and hours of spooling thread and of weaving with the single idea of producing a minimum number of lengths of cloth to deliver. If they didn't produce, they risked starva-tion—it was that simple! At my parents' and at my home, it was more bearable. My father was much more skilled than Auguste's father. That, to a degree, was what let them do better, although even they weren't rich. At least their poverty was less extreme.

As Saint Catherine's Day approached, I could hardly con-tain myself. My husband was finally going to return. I was on the embankment on the expected day of his return, long before he was supposed to arrive. I watched for the approach of the band of seasonal migrants.

It was very cold that year. The biting north wind that swept across the plain from Cambrai was trapped in our *coron*, where it swirled angrily, as if to avenge itself for being caught. I watched and watched, whipped by the wind, my eyes and face all red. Finally, there were the first of the returning band at the top of the slope. They trudged with heads low, so as not to offer too much resistance to the wind. I saw him in the middle of the group because he was taller than the others. He was wrapped up in his blanket and searching for me with his eyes. He saw me! Then he took off at such a gallop that he left the rest of the group as if they were standing still.

Ah! When I felt his arms close around me, I was warm again right away! My big one was there, spluttering with joy, enveloping me in his blanket. "How are you, Marie-Cat? How are you, Marie-Cat?" He repeated it over and over while I reassured him, "But yes, I'm fine. . . . And you? And you?"

We rediscovered each other during this dialogue in which each was completely occupied with the other, not listening to the answers. We felt as tender, as loving, as we were to be for the rest of our life together. Then finally he asked about the little one. It was like that always: I came before the child in his heart as, in mine, he was always first.

Arm in arm, we went back to the warmth of our cottage, where the soup boiled busily on the little stove, stuffed to the brim with briquettes. Auguste, who had hugged the baby for a long time, turning him round and round as if he was checking that he was all there, swallowed bowls and bowls of soup. He ate the whole kettleful of soup, as famished as he was tired from his long trip. I found him even thinner than before his departure, worn out by the life he had lived for seven months. He had been in the fields from dawn to night, struggling endlessly against the reluctant earth to make her give up her riches, in all weather, as though constantly in battle.

I took the evening off. After dinner, Auguste described his season in great detail. There had been awful weather, with continuous rain all spring, a harvest plagued by violent storms, so violent that the sheaves scattered like bits of straw. Reapers and bundlers had fled under the downpour, seized with that ancestral fear of murderous lightning. It was so stormy, Auguste told me, that one day out of two, one couldn't hear the Angelus at the neighborhood church. The Angelus was the moment when, all through our lives, my husband and I stopped our work for a few seconds of silence. We continued to observe the custom even after the church bells no longer rang the Angelus. The bad weather luckily hadn't prevented Auguste from bringing home a well-filled money bag. But at what price? Surely a very high one, I guessed from looking at his tanned and creased face, at his hands, which were even more knotty and crisscrossed with deep wrinkles than on his departure.

That evening, my husband fell asleep like a lump, in a moment, as soon as he got into bed. I had let him get into bed before me, as I felt that he was overcome with fatigue, and I was right. I held the lamp over his head and watched him sleep, like a corpse, almost greedily, as he had eaten. His big body was spread out under the covers to absorb the benefits of his deep sleep. He slept like that until 7:00 A.M., motionless except for his chest rising regularly, satiating himself with sleep, relaxed, home at last. He had no more worries about his family. I slid in next to him gently, taking up as little space as possible. When he woke up, I was already working at my loom. There were two big slices of bread spread with a layer of white cheese that was well salted and peppered on the table, just as he liked it. And his chicory was warming on the little stove.

Chapter Five

I had had a plan for quite a while—to find a larger house with a cellar where we could put our own looms, thus allowing us to live our life all on our own, without inconveniencing my parents. Now we had the chance. Some neighbors moved to join their children near Lyons. Their house was exactly like the one I had lived in as a child. We would have to pay five francs more per month, but given that we wouldn't have the coming and going to eat at home, we would save time.

Once we had the agreement of the landlord, we moved in our four pieces of furniture. As Auguste said, there was no need to get a mover for that. It was quickly done! A couple of days in advance, my husband whitewashed the walls inside the room and the cellar and carefully scrubbed the red tiled floor, which shone as if it had been waxed.

What joy to be finally all moved in! The two looms were set up in the cellar, where we had space to work. Paul came to help Auguste. My father gave me my loom as a present. He would hear nothing of it when I said I would pay him, because, after all, it belonged to him. Maman offered to continue preparing our yarn for us and that made me happy, for I was concerned about how that would be done. We gave her three francs a week for this task, which was fine all around.

The winter passed, and it was time for Auguste's next departure for the season. I still couldn't accompany him, but we both accepted this. As long as the baby needed me, it would be like that. While my husband was gone, I again worked extra hard, and we began to put a couple of sous aside. They were hidden in a pot full of flour, for fear of robbers. When I had a five-franc silver coin, I would put it in the pot, burying it in the white powder. We did that for a long time, and the money we did spend was always white and left traces of flour in our hands.

Auguste's letters—or rather those that he had written for him—marked the weeks of his absence. They came with the rhythm of the work and of the seasons. I was with him in thought; in my imagination we went together to the fields. It bothered me not to go, for I missed the fresh air. Little Auguste grew well. I often left him with my parents-in-law, who allowed me to bring some potatoes or a bit of salt pork in payment. They were happy to accept these little extras. On April 6, 1914, when our son was three, it was agreed that I would go again with my husband to the country. My parents-in-law would take care of the child, for which we paid them ten francs a month.

I was happy at the thought of returning to the Saint-Martin farm. How was I to guess that I was leaving Avesnes forever, or almost forever, that year? How could I suspect that I would never again see my poor mother; that a terrible upheaval would overturn our life, break up families, separate brothers from their sisters and children from their parents forever?

We knew nothing of the war clouds gathering in the east: they weren't clouds in our sky. Of course, the ladies from the château sometimes talked, at the baker's, of curious things happening in distant countries whose names sounded harsh and strange to my ears. Austria-Hungary, Serbia, Bosnia-

Herzegovina. There, outside our lives, a terrible drama took shape, one that would spread death, ruin, mourning even to our little village, so ignorant of what awaited it, so unconscious of the future. The villagers' only concerns were immediate: weaving, the harvest, gathering the sugar beets.

The weather was beautiful at dawn on the morning of May 5, when we left Avesnes to walk to the Cambrai railroad station twelve kilometers away. The day before, I had kissed my parents goodbye. Was it a presentiment? My mother seemed in worse health than ever before. She looked aged and tired. "If I don't see you again, 'our' Marie, remember your first-communion picture, which is in the box with our papers," she told me. I reassured her, laughing. But she was still concerned. She had felt the shadow of death pass over her head. We hugged our little one, chubby and smiling, for a long time. He was talking now, and religiously spoiled by his grandparents.

The Cambrai station, where we caught the train, seemed less gloomy than usual under the blue sky. Its long walls of red brick were brightened by beds of spring flowers, which would just have time to wither before being destroyed by German artillery shells.

After moving into the farm, we began the tasks we did each year. I remember each job so well—I can almost say with joy, even though they were not all pleasant. In the fields there was a great flood of workers, yearly workers and seasonal laborers, bent to their task amid the slow coming and going of the oxcarts. At harvest time, the Belgian reapers did not come. In the courtyard, I stared, foolishly, at the strange machine that had arrived the week before to replace them. It was an enormous, misshapen machine, covered with levers and handles, carrying long, keen points at ground level, which made it look like a weapon. It was a reaper-binder, the first I had ever seen in action, working hour after hour at the regular pace of the Ardennais horses that pulled it. The wheat fell miraculously before it; then it was caught, bundled, and finally dumped behind, where our job was simply to stack it.

That was what we were doing August 3, in the overpowering heat, surrounded by the strong odor of freshly cut hay and the sweat of the workers. Suddenly, at the neighborhood church, a furious, irregular, extraordinary bell-ringing broke out.

"The tocsin!" cried someone in the field. "There's a fire in the fields!" Then we saw men running and yelling on the road bordering the field. We couldn't hear what they were saying, but as they passed, the workers dropped their tools, running wildly, seized with some madness after a second of shock. Soon the field was swept with a wave of agitation. As the words reached them, people began running. My husband and I stared without understanding, before we heard, right in our faces, the news that a neighbor, in his turn, was yelling, "War! It's war!"

We were stunned. I remember that Auguste, turning toward me, said, "War, but what war?"

Then, we dropped our tools, the little hooks that we used to pile up the sheaves, and joined the crowd, running as fast as our legs could carry us, to the farmhouse. Everyone was going there, in the great need that men feel to gather together when faced with a catastrophe. In the courtyard, there was more excitement that I had ever seen there before. The men, usually so calm, usually so slow-moving, were seized with frenzy. Horses entered at a quick trot, whipped by their drivers, while the oxen, goaded until they bled, hurried in reluctantly. In this coming-and-going of wagons and animals, I could hear disjointed phrases: "General mobilization . . ." "What a misfortune, what an awful misfortune!" "I have to leave right away!" "Good God, where's my bundle?" "The Germans are attacking. . . ." "It was all bound to come to this. . . ."

The agent, pale as a sheet, succeeded in making himself

heard after a while. "It's serious, my friends, but we must keep calm. Those who must leave can do so right away. We'll pay them quickly."

Auguste didn't know where he stood. Luckily, in the papers that we always carried with us, I found the draft deferment he had received in Cambrai shortly before our marriage. He had come back from the medical board saying that they hadn't wanted him because he didn't weigh enough for his height. When Auguste spoke to the agent, who was preparing to go to the barracks himself, he advised Auguste to report to the military headquarters in Dieppe, the closest city.[1] Auguste went and stayed there two days before returning with a new deferment. Thus I was spared the anguish that I read in the eyes of most of the women around me. My husband wasn't going, though no one else knew why, because he was never sick. I must say that no one complained and no one questioned us about it. For the kilo he was missing, his life may have been saved. He surely avoided many sufferings.

We packed quickly, worried about what was happening to our parents and our child back in Avesnes. The preparation for our return trip took us several days, and when we arrived at the railroad station we had a real shock.

When we asked for tickets to Cambrai, the clerk shook his head and called the supervisor. The supervisor put on a serious look when he learned of our destination. "You can't go there, my poor children," he said. "The Cambrai station is in flames. It is being shelled." We felt homeless, crushed by the war, which was moving so quickly. Pushing rapidly through Belgium, the Germans were about to invade France. Our village, so close to the frontier, was one of the first to be taken.

We spent long months in anguish over the fate of our loved ones before learning that Auguste's parents had fled before the arrival of the Boches, taking our son to Brittany in a slow voyage by horse-drawn wagon, driven by a helpful farmer. My parents had stayed in Avesnes.

For the moment, we returned to the Saint-Martin farm. Every day more of the men left, but the women all stayed, like us, turned back by the railroad clerks, who refused to let them leave in order to avoid slowing traffic. Besides, where could they go? Most were from our region. They would have found their way blocked kilometers from their homes. At the farm, at least, they had a roof over their heads and bread to eat.

The agent, who was getting ready himself to go to fight, called my husband into his office. "Santerre, I trust you, you are a good worker. Because you are able and can stay, I am entrusting the rest of the harvest to you. Do the best you can with the workers who have stayed behind. You can manage!"

Auguste managed, but not without plenty of trouble. He had to finish the partially completed harvest with women, young men who weren't yet drafted, and the folks who were too old to be drafted. He learned to drive the bladed monster that reaped the wheat. And he worked the miracle. At the beginning of September, the wheat was all stored in the barns, for better or for worse. The only loss was some of the sugar beets, harvested later. The people left behind worked as hard as they could, but they couldn't replace the strong arms of the men who were already fighting and dying far away.

In November, we got a letter from Paris. It was from the agricultural company that employed us. They wrote my husband that he should move to Avay, to live near the sugar refinery there and help run the factory. We moved into a very comfortable lodging of four rooms which the company assigned to us. I took my carefully set-aside savings and we bought some furniture and a cookstove.

If it hadn't been for not knowing the fate of my loved ones, my son above all, I would have been perfectly happy then. Instead, what a nightmare it was those next weeks! I would wake in a sweat, having dreamed that my little one had been buried in the ruins of the house, or that he had been captured by the Germans . . . or even worse, that the soldiers had cut his throat. Such awful stories were going around about the enemy soldiers that people were panic-stricken. They said that the soldiers cut boys' hands off to keep them from fighting in the future and that they sliced off women's breasts so that they couldn't nurse babies. With such specific, horrible details, we believed what we heard. It was hard to sleep. What a relief when we got a letter from Saint-Quay in Britanny. My parents-in-law sent word that they had finally gotten there after the German invasion of the Nord. They described their terrible long flight in a wagon with the farmer who had sold us meat in the past.

Many people of the Nord fled the invaders as my parents-in-law did, with horses, oxen, handcarts, wheelbarrows—whole crowds of poor people. Some left so quickly that they fled with empty hands. And among the crowds of people were the animals: cows, sheep, goats, donkeys, driven by their owners in unbelievable disorder. The frightened crowd had more than once found its way barred by French army barricades. The refugees had detoured down country roads, obscure roads where they got lost, or were stranded at isolated farms where there wasn't room for so many people. Then they were sent on, always farther away.

Near Amiens, the farmer, in despair, was ready to quit trying to go any farther. There the horde of refugees got all mixed up with divisions of the French army, who were headed for the front. At first, it was the infantry, and that wasn't so bad. But then, the artillery rolled up, and the mess was really scary: the huge agricultural wagons got tangled with the heavy harnesses of the caissons and military wagons in an awful jumble. The gunners, known for their love of correctness and order, swore like heathens before this unexpected hindrance, which was slowing their march toward the front. Worst of all in that mess were the fights between horses. The solid Ardennais or Percherons of the farmers fought the nervous, quick horses of the artillery. They grabbed at each other's manes in passing, with desperate whinnies, while their masters shouted insults or even struck at each other.

It wasn't until they got near Rouen that the refugees—here and there, they were already called "émigrés"—finally found relative calm. From then on, their voyage toward Britanny continued at a more routine pace. The old Santerres, who had never before left their village, never recovered from the confusing and frightening experience. They were bewildered by the unknown landscape before their eyes; it was like a country that they couldn't ever get used to.

The letter they mailed us, full of details, was written by a woman teacher from Saint-Quay whom they had met. She had "adopted" little Auguste, who, she told us, was doing well. He was sturdy and talkative, and benefiting from the country air of Brittany.

We mailed a money order of twenty francs—all we had left—to the old Santerres in Britanny, who were broke. Then Auguste and I decided to go to Saint-Quay to fetch them and bring them back to our lodgings.

My husband was unhappy, knowing that his parents were penniless. But there was a problem. We didn't have any more money. I confided in the agent's wife. I was helping at the farmhouse with cooking, housework, laundry. I hardly ever went to the fields in the winter. Instead, I walked every day to her house from Avay, where we lived.

Later, around the beginning of January 1915, she gave us a hundred francs. "This," she told us, "is a bonus from the company to reward your husband for his hard work in the harvests." At the beginning of February we left, taking advantage of the slow season to get a couple of days off. What a trip! We had to from Dieppe to Paris, and from Paris to Brest.

At the Saint-Lazare railroad station in Paris, we were almost swept away by the vast crowd of travelers. The huge waiting room swarmed with soldiers. We had never seen so many people. They spoke of but one thing, the war. The war was the main topic of conversation on the train that took us to Brittany as well. Soldiers on leave, wounded soldiers with arms in slings, faces covered with bandages, told of horrors. The Germans, they said, had begun using poison gas up north, in the Aisne and the Nord, our province. Their voices trembled with fear as they described that infernal invention. It killed those who breathed it a little bit at a time, messily, with rotted lungs. They lay on hospital beds, screaming with pain and begging to be delivered from it. Nothing could be done for them.

What an awful time! Secretly, I rejoiced, a bit selfishly, that Auguste had escaped all these abominations!

We found our son and my parents-in-law at Saint-Quay, all in good health. They were wild with joy to see us again. Ah, how different the grandfather was from his former surly self! He cried to see us again, like a child, in long painful sobs which we couldn't comfort or stop. We left as soon as they had packed. We couldn't afford to take too much time off.

We brought everyone back to Avay and settled the Santerres temporarily in our apartment before the company authorized us to lodge them in a furnished room at the farm.

The elder Santerres depended on us for the rest of their lives. The poor things didn't cost us much! They were used to living simply, like monks, so they never complained at all. They were content with little, very little. Nevertheless, they were a burden for us. We never forgot what they had done for our little one and we saw that they had all that they needed. Besides, for a long time they were able to be really helpful. They took care of our son, and the grandfather carved out a bit of garden behind the farm, in which he grew heaps of vegetables. The grandmother mended my linen with incredible care and patience. The more we urged them to rest, the more they devoted themselves to work. Since they were used to not paying attention to themselves, they simply drove themselves to the limits of their strength.

What a sad Christmas we had in 1915! In the church at Avay, there were only women and old people at midnight mass. We saw some men on leave in the choir, mostly wounded soldiers. The priest urged us all to have courage and resignation in that abominable time. I thought about my parents and prayed for them. Memories of my childhood flooded back. I missed my parents and was worried about Maman. How could I know then that my poor mother had been dead for more than four months? I didn't hear about her death until later, in February 1916. I received a letter marked with a red cross, with the inscription "Occupied Territories Mail." The letter was well written, clear, and very long. It was from the new priest of Avesnes—the old one had died.

In it, he described what had happened to my mother in great detail. At the beginning of the war, my brother Léandre, who lived in Cambrai, was called up. His departure, followed soon after by that of Paul, Lucie's husband, plus our absence began to wear on Maman, already aged and very tired. She worried about all of us. The worst problem was that she had no news and no chance of getting any in the unbelievable disorder that followed the declaration of war. Like my father, she couldn't read, which isolated her from much of the news. Totally contradictory information was flying by word of mouth.

So it was that she heard an awful rumor toward the end of 1914. My brother Léandre, someone told her, had been killed in the Argonne. Who told her that news? No one knows, no one ever knew. Not a single official paper confirmed this death, but it was the crowning blow for my mother. Her second son was gone too. The first, burned alive as a child, and now this one torn from her, doubtless dying in an equally cruel way.

The poor woman was beside herself, and she began to fall apart. For what had she worked all her life, not even knowing what she would eat the next day? Now the children who had been the only joy of her life were being stolen from her, snatched from her home or buried in the crater of a shell. My father, weakened physically, wasn't much comfort to her. He could not comprehend all that had happened. His sole concern was the loom on which he continued to weave for hours and hours, from a habit too old to die. Praise God, they had that, so they could eat. In fact, the company that employed them had started to do business again right away with the Germans, and orders still flowed in.

The new priest, very young and not well himself, new to his post in Avesnes, was overwhelmed by this drama. He was horrified by their miserable existence, this dog's existence. One day, mother, exhausted, prostrated with sorrow, lay down in the main room. She never again left the bed on which she had brought thirteen children into the world. All those children except Lucie, who had stayed near her, were scattered or dead. She had lost the courage that she had shown us her whole life long.

The priest's letter continued the story: "One Monday morning, two women from the Red Cross came into the house. They were happy, and waved a piece of paper: 'Madame Gardez, Madame Gardez, we have news of your son Léandre! He is doing as well as possible. He is a prisoner in Silesia.' " But our mother seemed not to hear. She was white as a sheet, and she didn't move. She died that evening at 9:00.

I was crushed. So Maman had died. She had lain buried in the little cemetery for a long time and I hadn't even known. Poor Maman. I heard her whisper in my ear again: "Our Marie, remember your first-communion picture, which is in the box with our papers." And going back even further, to the day I became a woman: "You know that each month your Papa doesn't sleep in bed for a few days but on the floor, rolled up in a blanket."

She was sixty-eight when God took her to Him. Those days

are long past, but I've never forgotten my mother. She was a saint, the kind of woman that isn't made anymore. Her only consolation in the end was the same as mine now. She had been happy with my father because their hard—and sometimes miserable—life was sweetened by an undying tenderness at all times, with misfortunes and joys shared every minute, every second.

The end of the war surprised us as much as the beginning. It had lasted so long that we stopped believing it would end someday. So when the carillon at the Avay church began to ring joyously in November 1918, we didn't know what it meant. Joy spread throught the streets of the village. Women went out on their doorsteps, children ran by yelling, and old people wept in the streets like kids.

My father-in-law was one of the first to hear the news. Despite his age, he had been employed for several months by the commune. There weren't enough men to clean the streets and bury people. He came to us transfigured. He didn't know yet that one of his sons had died several days before in the gunfire at the Navarrin farm. That news was part of the sad lot the future brought us. There was mourning for the dead and sorrow about the wounded. The agricultural laborers came back as amputees, blind, gassed, or as "scar throats," as some were called because of their disfigured, crudely healed faces. We began to see more and more returning. What a crowd! What a rude shock at the railroad station, where the wives went to meet their husbands, to find them like that—crippled, sick, despairing that they would be of no use anymore. At first, we had the impression that all those returning had been injured. It wasn't until later that those who had escaped without a scratch returned. But, like their comrades, they were serious, sad, unsmiling; they spoke little. They had lived in hell for four years and wouldn't forget it.

Soon after the Armistice, Auguste and I decided to go

home to Avesnes. We were anxious to return to our house in the *coron* and to see my father again. We sold our furnishings quickly: dishes, linen, and all. We saved only bare necessities. This time, we were able to buy the tickets to Cambrai that we had been denied four years earlier. How long the journey seemed!

Finally, there was the railroad station at Cambrai, still a pile of scattered bricks. Auguste wanted to take the cab, "the mail," which would drop us off at the base of "our" embankment.

How moving it was to see those familiar sights, unchanged, or so it seemed! Then—when we tried to turn the key in our lock, it was blocked. The door of our cottage opened. A woman we didn't know was on the threshold. Inside, children cried, and a whiff of bad-smelling air drifted toward us. We explained bit by bit, but it wasn't easy. Finally, we had to face the truth. This family had rented our house, but empty, empty of everything! No more furniture, no more stove—nothing. No, something remained. On one of the broken window-panes, I saw with a terrible wrench of my heart the holy picture I had received at my first communion. Who had stuck it there? My mother, perhaps? I didn't know then, and I never have known. But it was my picture, an image of the Virgin with one corner, the upper right one, torn off, and my first name written at the bottom by the old priest.

At the town hall, we found out what the situation was and learned at the same time that Papa no longer lived in Avesnes. Several months before, he had been sent to the old-age home in Etaples.

So we had nothing. Everything was gone. Our poor little cottage had been looted by the Germans. Nothing re-mained—not a stick of furniture, not a dish, not a sheet, not a bit of string. And Papa was gone too.

My head was spinning at all the disasters I had found out about in quick succession. Auguste stood beside me, over-come and silent. Then we thought of Lucie. A child played before her door. I recognized him; it was Alfred, my godson, but how he had grown! And in the room, a woman in black whom I didn't recognize. But she came toward us, smiling. My husband and I were shocked. It was Lucie, but in what a state! She was emaciated, her hair was white! Stupidly, unsuspectingly, we asked after Paul. I thought she was in mourning for Maman. We learned then that my brother-in-law had been killed at Fère-en-Tardenois in 1916, trapped in a communication tunnel.

We were filled with sorrow. Nothing was as expected. Everything had changed, even, it seemed, our *coron*. The baker, Arsène, was dead too, shot by the Germans for refusing to bake bread for the troops passing through. Practically nothing familiar remained. The next day, after spending the night at Lucie's house, we went to Etaples to see Papa. Again, despair. Was this my father, this man with white hair, whose beard had been shaved off? This man who barely recognized us and showed no pleasure at our visit? He roused himself and smiled weakly only when we said that we would take him to Avesnes to visit Maman's grave.

In the little cemetery, there came the final shock. It had been shelled, and the burial vaults were destroyed. We could see uprooted coffins in the frightful chaos, splintered by shrapnel and mixed with bits of funerary wreaths. Crosses of stone or wood, monuments—which, it's true, were rare—had been tumbled down by the explosions and scattered about, as if by a giant hand. Thanks to Papa, we were able to find ourselves in the mess. Maman's tomb, which was close to a wall, had been partly spared. But the big oaken cross had been slashed by a shell, just where the name and date were carved. Too much, it was too much! I felt defeated; I couldn't face up to all this sorrow and shock. I fell to the ground, weeping loudly. What had we done to our good Lord to make Him punish us this way? I sobbed desperately. My husband and father stood by silently, overcome also, with tears in their eyes.

We heard a hesitant step behind us. It was the new priest, a young man with a limp. We introduced ourselves, thanking him for his long letter. He saw my despair and read in my eyes the terrible doubt that had seized me, for the first time in my life. "It's a time of great misery for all," he said, and his voice, very gentle, echoed in an odd way in the ruined cemetery. "But despite our misfortunes, we must keep on hoping. Remember that others suffer still more."

We watched him leave, walking painfully among heaps of earth thrown up by the shells. He stopped for a moment and straightened a fallen cross. Then he began walking again, as if discouraged by the useless gesture he had made. Everything in that holy ground would have to be rebuilt. He left as he had come, hobbling slowly.

Returning to Lucie's house, Auguste and I discussed the situation. Since there was no one and nothing of ours left in Avesnes, wouldn't it be best to return to Avay? That was what we did in the end, after trying in vain to persuade my father to come. He refused firmly, in a final show of authority. He wanted to stay there, in the old-age home, where he was well cared for and close to his wife; he could visit her in the cemetery when he wanted to. I never saw my mother's grave, or my father either, again. He died on a summer evening, from chills and fever, caught on a visit to the cemetery. It was 1920, and I couldn't go to the funeral because it was the height of the harvest season. My poor little village of Avesnes! I left it forever that day, and with it all that was dear to me. So many memories were born there: those of my childhood, of my vanished parents, of all that the war had snatched away so cruelly.

Luckily, I still had my two Augustes. My life continued with them until they, too, were taken from me.

Chapter Six

I n Avay, we happily rejoined our son. He was nine then, and we were going to send him to school. He often missed his good friend "the teacher," whom he saw no more, and for good reason. The man Auguste called his teacher was one of the German prisoners who had been brought to the farm to work in the fields. He had stayed in Saint-Martin for three years. Little by little, a bond of friendship had formed between him and Auguste, whom he called "Gust." The German taught him how to read and write a little. One day he had drawn his portrait from a little photo.

The German had gone back to his homeland, and young Auguste was very sad at his departure. Maybe that was why he refused to go to school. I couldn't get him to obey me, so I resorted to the strap, which shamed him when I took him to class. Then he escaped me and ran home. His father had to take a hand in the affair. And my Auguste didn't joke around. He himself had no schooling, so he felt even more strongly that his son should not lose out the same way.

The company took us back into its service without questions when we returned from Avesnes. They gave us another apartment, larger than the one we had before. But we had to buy furniture, linen, and dishes again. For two weeks, my husband watched the sales and we reequipped ourselves as well as possible. From then on, Auguste spent most of his time at the sugar refinery. When the harvests were in full swing, he would go back to the farm itself, but as a wagon driver.

For the rest of the time we lived in Avay, neither he nor I returned to field work. I helped the agent's wife, as during the war years. Her husband had returned safe and sound. My life was much easier, but I had plenty to do. I had to cook, do the dishes, wash enormous mountains of laundry that included the bedsheets of all the farm workers, and clean. I was busy from 8:00 in the morning until 9:00 in the evening. The food was good, though. For the first time in my life, I ate meat at almost every meal, and that seemed wonderful to me. When I churned the butter for her, my boss sometimes gave me a litle pot of cream.

When Auguste worked at the sugar refinery, he had to cook for himself and the little one. We didn't see each other during the day, as we worked two kilometers apart. He also had very long, hard days, twelve or thirteen hours, seven days a week. When the sugar was being made, he worked the night shift. From evening to dawn, he used a wooden shovel to ladle the boiling sugar, in a white rain of sweet drops, into the cooling vats. He came home at dawn, dog-tired, hardly able to walk straight. When I kissed him, I licked his cheeks playfully, for they were sugar-coated.

The thing that impressed me most in my work in the kitchen was the meals we prepared for the servants, in quantities that seemed colossal: peeled potatoes boiled over the fire in full laundry tubs; pieces of meat so large they could have fed my whole village for a week.

The meat, slaughtered at the farm, arrived in the kitchen in quarters of beef. To my dismay, one of these would be eaten at a single meal! The strapping farm laborers ate and swallowed in religious silence, slowly chewing their enormous mouthfuls and rolling their bread into balls between their big gnarled fingers. The poor farm dogs got nothing but bones at the end of those meals, and those bones had been scraped clean with knives and sucked of their marrow.

I wasn't used to such orgies of eating, and I sometimes was stopped in my tracks as I served, dumbfounded to see so much food disappear at one time. The farm workers ate three meals a day, and four in summer. The pots of meat never stopped simmering and browning.

Pot roasts, stews, soups were served by the ladleful in big earthenware basins that returned to us so cleanly emptied that we sometimes wondered if we had washed them twice by mistake.

On Sunday, there was red meat or poultry, big pieces of beef swimming in blood, which were shoveled into the huge stone oven over the fireplace where tree trunks burned with searing heat. When we served chicken, there was a veritable massacre in the poultry yard, starting at dawn. Knife in hand, servants would run after their chosen victims, which they then plucked clean. And for half an hour we heard the desperate cackling of the birds and the helpless flapping of their clipped wings.

I had a hard time getting used to these "snacks," as they were called in Normandy. In my childhood, the simplicity of our table had been such that this flood of food seemed like a waste. The farm laborers weren't cheating on food! They needed that much nourishment to work for hours that are unimaginable these days. These schedules exhausted them to a point where many of them were too tired to undress when night came and they threw themselves on their beds as though dead, snoring through open mouths. Early in the morning the next day, they had to pull themselves out of bed to work again.

They woke themselves up by plunging into the water at the pump, right up to their stomachs, snorting like the farm animals. In the winter, they sometimes had to break the ice in the trough by kicking it with their sabots before drenching themselves without a shiver. Yes, they were rough men, to be sure, but good on the whole. Whenever I passed one as I carried my buckets of water from the well, he would take my burden silently and carry it to the kitchen.

I knew their work well and how tough it was. None of them ever complained. During the threshing, before the machines took their place, they would line up in the morning in two ranks in the courtyard, with the wheat to be threshed between them. With the long handles of their flails on their shoulders, they looked like a regiment of soldiers at attention. Then the foreman stood at the head of the two lines. With a voice that grew hoarser as the hours passed, he set the rhythm that controlled the movement of the flails: "Up—down . . . Up—down!"

The long wooden handles whipped through the air for seconds with a whistling sound before falling with a dry smack on the ears of wheat that they pulverized in a puff of golden dust. This task was dangerous, and it required a well-experienced team, used to the work; the agent supervised personally. The flails had to be maneuvered by sure hands so that they didn't crush their neighbors or cut off their ears in passing. These men were not only brave but highly skilled.

One Sunday morning, Auguste, my son, arrived at the farm on a run. He told me that his Grandmother Santerre had just died suddenly. She was seventy-two years old. With the permission of my boss, I went right back to the village and then to the sugar refinery, to tell my husband the news. But he couldn't get off work and didn't see his father until that evening. Sitting in the little apartment which the village had assigned to my in-laws, Santerre was completely overcome. He wrestled with the enormity of the fact that for the first time in half a century his wife was no longer beside him. He couldn't believe it. He stared, dazed, at the inert corpse of his wife on the bed. He gazed for a moment at the stiff face which, it seemed, had paradoxically been rejuvenated by death. "What a dog's life!" he said. "She is well rid of it, my poor old one." He began to cry softly, his head in his hands. Distant memories came back to his mind. Marriage, the birth of children, the long hours of work together, the difficulties they faced each day of feeding all those kids. She had been with him constantly, silent but always helping.

My father-in-law had never been gentle. Did he have regrets now? He never shook the depression into which his wife's death plunged him. He couldn't get over his loss. One month later, practically to the day, he died in turn. Suddenly, like his wife. We found him stretched out on his bed. That was a very difficult time for my husband. His parents had been cruel and unfair to him, but he forgot all that in those painful times. He refused to harp on his grievances. Our son too felt the loss deeply. He loved his Pépé and Mémé Santerre, who had cared for him for so many years.

It was about that time my husband became a volunteer fireman. The village fire company was being reorganized; they had broken up because of the war and the loss of so many men. Now young men were recruited to join the older ones who had returned from the war. The mayor came to our house one evening. I hadn't come home yet, but Auguste told me the news when I returned later. At first I didn't like it at all. My husband had plenty of work without accepting this responsibility on top of it. But my opinion made no difference. He thought it natural to go, saying that someone had to be there when they needed help.

Firefighters were really needed, for there were many fires in the region. They were hard to put out, and often became real dramas. As soon as a fire was discovered, of course, everyone ran to it, but often there was nothing to be done. There wasn't enough water for the bucket lines that we made. The fires were a true plague.

The worst were after the harvest. Haystacks, overstuffed barns were quick to burn. Most of the time, it was the fault of a careless tramp, smoking in the hay where he was sleeping, or of a negligent farm worker. Often all that could be done was to save the neighboring buildings, because nothing could save the place that caught fire.

That was why the prefecture ordered the communes to reorganize their fire companies. Auguste received a uniform, and he looked superb when he wore it. The village firemen had a magnificent hand pump whose copper body gleamed like the pots and pans in my kitchen. Today, when I see the enormous trucks and the equipment that go into action when the sirens sound, I can't help thinking of the Avay company: their little pumper and their fierce struggles against fires. Suprisingly enough, the hand pump was very effective. Mostly, it let the men hold off the flames while waiting for help from the neighboring town, which sometimes arrived several hours later. They had a big steam engine with a clanging bell, pulled by four galloping horses, which roused the countryside as it rumbled through.

After he became a fireman, my husband had to get up nights many times. Someone ran and knocked at the door when he was needed: the fire chief rushed around the whole village to collect his men. But usually they were already up, awakened by the desperate call of the tocsin at the church. In an agricultural region like that, fire was the number one enemy, an enemy that in an hour could turn weeks, months, or years of work into ashes.

I could never relax when my husband went off like that. I had worries, dark worries. He'd come back black as a charcoal burner and worn out from his unequal struggle with fire. Then he had to go to his work at the refinery the next day.

One time was especially frightening. That evening, Auguste came home from the refinery in a dreadful storm. We heard the wind tearing tiles off the roofs and smashing them on the cobblestones of the road like gunshots.

"Well," my husband said as he lay down, "no mold will grow in the fields tonight." It was October and, luckily, the harvest had been safely stored in the barns, which comforted us to a certain degree. "It's really going to town out there," muttered Auguste, who was tossing and turning, unable to sleep in this racket.

Finally, sleep enveloped us. Not for long. I felt myself shaken suddenly; it was my husband. "Listen, Marie-Cat," he said in my ear. Over the screaming tempest, the sound of pealing bells came from the church nearby. I wondered how I could have missed it. I must have been tired! "The tocsin, it's the tocsin!" Auguste cried, jumping out of bed.

The tocsin! It was the tocsin that marked the bad times, the great disasters in our region. It was never good news when the priest pulled on the bell ropes that way, pulling them all together, with all his strength. The bells rang in an uncontrolled, frantic rhythm, in no particular order, randomly, creating an impression of panic in and of themselves. The tocsin! For centuries upon centuries it was the sole form of rapid communication for the isolated peasant. From one church to another, from bell tower to bell tower, news of misfortune swept through the fields, announcing invasion, fire, flood, epidemic. The desperate sound of the tocsin disturbed the traditional calm of field labor, calling the peasant back to his endangered home.

Auguste dressed quickly. Just at that moment, we heard violent knocking on the door. It was Cluchon, the sergeant, who was calling my husband: "Santerre, hurry, in the name of God! The Obiers farm is burning!" The Obiers farm was at the edge of Avay on the plain. Its buildings were an old fort that had been built there to defend the entry to the village. They were vast stone buildings constructed in a square around an immense court that was closed in the evening by a single huge door. It took two people to move it.

Accompanied by the screaming wind, we heard coming and going, yelling in the streets. This was soon followed by the sounds of galloping horses that were being rushed to be harnessed to cisterns full of water. The news was spreading through the settlement: "The Obiers is burning, the Obiers is burning!" A fire at Obiers meant that the village was in danger. Cursing farmers woke their frightened laborers, and wagons were dragged out of their barns, the horses wakened by whiplashes, all running toward the edge of the village. There one could already see a vast blood-red glow and thick clouds of smoke.

An hour passed. The storm continued with such violence that it seemed like it wouldn't end for quite a while. I couldn't stand it any longer; I was sick with worry. I dressed my son warmly and we set off through the village streets. We ran to the old barracks. There I stopped, stunned, breathless. The five farm buildings were flaming like matches right through their slate roofs. The fire crackled noisily as the wind continued to stir up the flames wickedly. Enormous crossbeams crashed and fell in a shower of sparks.

But what was so frightful—amid all that—was the frightened shrieks of the trapped animals, the milk cows, the calves, the cattle, the sheep, the pigs of that vast enterprise. No one had had time to free them from their stalls, because of the suddenness of the disaster. Those poor trapped animals! Many died that night, for they couldn't be freed. Those that were able to break their tethers were a serious danger to the firefighters. The farmers themselves had to shoot the animals, their eyes all bloodshot as they ran in every direction. Orders crossed or were contradictory as they were drowned out in the awful din of horses' whinnies and the clanking sound of the iron cisterns full of water that were being dragged to the farm from farther and farther away. As the news spread, farmers were bringing water, a sign of their solidarity in the face of the misfortune of their fellow. After all, who knew where fire would strike tomorrow?

In the chaos, I looked in vain for Auguste, my husband. Finally, near the house, I found the hand pump, which four men were pushing rhythmically. Poor pump! It had never seemed as small as that night, in the glow of the immense flames rising in the sky.

I caught sight of Cluchon, the sergeant, who was losing his head in the gigantic disaster. He had organized bucket chains here and there, but now all converged on the house, which they were trying to save.

It seemed as though I had been there for hours before I heard the loud bell of the big emergency trucks of the neighboring village, arriving at last, pulled by four horses, white with sweat and spittle. The firemen were hanging on all along the sides of the pump, wearing their chenille helmets, as if at a parade. They were strictly organized, as a unit. The officer who commanded the firemen, a tall, straight man with metal-rimmed eyeglasses, gave brief orders that were easily heard in spite of the wind. The huge wagons positioned themselves at a gallop in the courtyard, which had first been systematically cleared by the men. The pressure pumps began to spray water through enormous hoses. Ah! if those people had been there earlier! Now, all they could do was soak the hissing and smoking embers.

I finally recovered my husband. The officer, in a rude tone of voice, made him come down from his ladder. "That wall will collapse in less than one minute," he said dryly to Cluchon, who was relieved to see the reinforcements finally arrive. What he said was true. The ladder had just been taken down when the wall fell in a rain of water and coals. I hugged Auguste against me. I wanted to kiss the officer, whose lenses shone in the glow of the last of the fire.

The fire at the Obiers farm did much damage and people

talked about it for a long time. It took many years for the farm to be completely rebuilt. The next July 14,[1] Auguste, pale in his handsome blue-and-red uniform, received a medal from a man in a dress suit who was in charge of giving out the awards. Someone said he was the subprefect. I was proud of Auguste that day, but I didn't forget my earlier feeling of fear. I was worried again more than once, but I must say that there never was another fire in a class with that one.

I was thirty when I began to have my pains for the first time. They seized me one day in the kitchen at the farm, where I was carrying a basin of hot water. A fierce pain stabbed my side and I almost fell on the tiles. Then the pain stopped as quickly as it had come, and I thought no more of it. But several days later it began again, and, worried, I told Auguste about it. He decided that we should go to Dieppe to see a doctor.

We went one morning in a wagon belonging to the farm that was delivering grain to the train station. The doctor examined me at length, which bothered me and didn't please Auguste at all. He gave me some pills to take, along with a powder. He didn't know what was wrong, I could see. For a while, it seemed as though the pains diminished a bit. Then they became more severe again. My work became torture, but I didn't want to stop, although Auguste advised me every day to do so. It was finally my boss who forced my hand. "You can't keep on like this, Marie-Catherine," she told me one day after lunch. "You can't even stand up straight." By that time, I was in constant pain.

We decided to change doctors. The new one saw right away what was wrong and advised us to go directly to the hospital in Rouen. The specialist—his name was Jane—who examined me prescribed an immediate operation. So I stayed there that very day. Auguste went home by himself, anxious and concerned, and I awaited the surgeon's knife. He removed a cyst from my left ovary, the cause of all my sufferings, without my feeling a twinge. Before the operation, I breathed the strong odor of ether to put me to sleep. I stayed at the hospital for a month and a half, with only one visit from my husband and my son, who was growing into a handsome fellow.

But a new sorrow came when I left the hospital. Professor Jane, who liked me very much, called Auguste and me into his office for a few minutes. He explained that we couldn't have any more children. It was finished: I couldn't believe it! We had very much wanted other kids, not many, as in my family, but at least three. Especially because, by then, we were better off materially. The return to Avay was made in silence. I was happy to have been cured of my sickness but sad to know that I couldn't have another baby.

I stayed home for the following months. My husband didn't want me to work, and that let me spend a little time with our son, Auguste, who quickly became all the dearer to us since we knew he would be the only one.

Little Auguste was working well at school. His teacher was pleased with him. But he never liked studying. When he turned thirteen, he entered an apprenticeship with Berger, the barber in Avay, a good man, very fat and mustachioed, who shaved and cut the hair of people from three kilometers around. He toured the neighboring villages in a little donkey cart and his arrival was an event.

Peasants went to the barber only on rare occasions. It was truly a luxury. But there eventually came the time when they had to indulge. And they would enter, silent, into one of the café rooms where Berger would set up shop. He scraped the rough leather of their cheeks and cut the manes of his clients with big snips of his scissors. As he was a real gossip, he would pass along the latest news of the region at the same time. He did it with such verve that the most insignificant information took on great proportions. The clients, their faces white with soap and their heads tilted back under the barber's big hands, listened closely so as not to miss a word of his inexhaustible gossip. Deaths, births, divorces, bad harvests—all important events in life were passed along by the fat Berger as he brushed and cut. Then, with a little amusing flourish, he would pocket three francs. He earned a good living with this work, which took him out of Avay and into smaller villages most of the time.

On Saturday or Sunday, he would stop in our village, where he had a barbershop in a room of his little house. It smelled good, of eau de cologne and shaving soap. There were two big revolving leather chairs and a table with a big porcelain basin into which clients plunged their faces to their noses, snorting, after he had trimmed their beards. Berger seasoned his barbering with the story of someone's life.

The face of that fat man was so extraordinary that I have never forgotten it. For the births of Peter's or Paul's children, he arranged his face to look joyful, curling his mustache. On the other hand, when he described a death, he seemed to be wearing mourning and his face was greatly afflicted. His eyes shone ironically when he told of the disappointments of a couple. He knew the most intimate, the most secret details, without anyone knowing how he learned them.

My son learned the barber's trade from Berger, and the two soon became a pair. People went to Auguste for their beards, because he had a gentler hand than his boss, which wasn't surprising. Some farmers, though pressed for time, preferred to wait for my son because he shaved them less roughly and sharpened their razors more carefully. At that time, each client had his own razor, with his name written above it, hanging from a board on the wall. And each brought his own towel for cleanliness.

Thus it was that Auguste—whom I always called the little one, to distinguish him from his father—grew up and became a young man. Everything was going well and he had begun to earn a few sous when one of my nieces wrote to us and then came to visit.

She was the daughter of my sister Edwige, and she was from the Seine-et-Marne, where she lived with her husband, a war cripple. The husband had become a cobbler when he returned from the front with a wooden leg that kept him from walking very well. My niece wasn't especially happy at home, which didn't keep her from wanting to help others. In fact, perhaps it made her want to help people even against their will. I had no idea, when she arrived, to what a degree she would change our life.

As soon as she saw our son, she took an interest in him and his work. At Mitry, in Brie,[2] where she lived, the barber was looking for an assistant, a good worker like Auguste who shaved so well. She succeeded in persuading him to return there with her to make his fortune.

And that was that—his father and I were left alone in Avay, saddened by the departure of little Auguste, who had filled such a place in our house, in our life. We couldn't get used to it. We kept expecting to see him; we wanted to talk to him.

It wasn't enough that both of us should have lost our parents in the preceding years. Now our son was gone too. We felt as if he too were dead, we missed him so much. That was 1929, which was one of the most painful years of my life. My little one was gone. It was hard to bear.

Chapter Seven

I got a letter from Auguste two weeks after his departure. In this first letter he described at length his move to Mitry. He told us about his work with the local barber. It was different there from his apprenticeship with the itinerant barber Berger and his tours around the countryside. He stayed in the salon all day long. There was a large clientele that came and went. With his tips, my son earned a decent wage, and he was very pleased. "The only problem," he wrote, "is that I worry about you, my dear parents. I miss you and our house, so calm and quiet, where no one shouts or argues."

He confided in us about life with his cousins, where he was lodging. It was very disrupted. My niece's husband, the cobbler, couldn't get over having lost a leg in the war. And, more and more, he drank to forget it. Auguste described how family fights would follow, especially at the end of the day, when the cobbler was drunk. Terrible quarrels! The husband broke everything in his shop and threw shoes waiting to be repaired all around the room, like a lunatic. When he had finished with objects, he would turn on his wife, whom he abused with abominable words, the worst filth my son had ever heard. It was hell.

I was dismayed, and my husband was too when I read him the letter. It was our first close encounter with alcoholism. At my parents' house, as at his, no one had ever tasted wine or hard liquor. It was partly out of custom, but also because it was much too costly. My father really hated liquor. "Alcohol in a house," Papa would say, "is the worst thing. It is laziness and filth which moves in on one. Once you've tried it you can never give it up."

I was lucky enough to be married to a man who felt the same way. During our life together, I never saw him drunk, not even tipsy. Pépé had a horror of wine, and, at the family celebrations we attended for over a half-century, he never took any, unflinchingly putting up with the teasing of the others, who said he was a sissy. Auguste sometimes got angry when we were out and someone taunted him too much. The discussion always ended there. Our son was like us. I understood his dislike of the daily spectacle at the cobbler's. It must have been very difficult.

About that time, feeling recovered and well rested, I began working at the farm again. The agent's wife welcomed me happily. She liked me a lot, and we understood each other perfectly. As long as I worked, I didn't miss my son as much. I had been bored at Avay, at home, restless for hours and hours, not knowing what to do! My house was quickly cleaned, and the rest of the day I was a lost soul.

One day while I was explaining all that to my boss, I mentioned the name of the city where Auguste was, in the Seine-et-Marne. "You mean he's at Mitry?" she cried. "What a coincidence! The company that we work for also has a farm and sugar refinery there!"

I couldn't believe my ears. She gave me more details. The company owned several big enterprises, mostly in the region of Paris. That meant hectares and hectares of land cultivated by seasonal laborers under the direction of agents, each responsible for a region. "There are thousands of people who work for the company just like you, Marie-Catherine."

The company had its headquarters in Paris, and none of the workers ever saw the owners. I saw one only once in Avay; he had come after an accident at the refinery, in a handsome black car with a chauffeur. He wore a frock coat and top hat. The visit of this serious man in black amazed the workers, for they had never talked to anyone but the agent, and then only briefly, in short snatches. Now the agent himself almost shook with fear when the director-general visited the refinery. Then the automobile left again, at full speed.

My boss continued to explain things that interested me very much: the company produced only wheat and sugar. From the immense plains of Normandy, the Beauce, and Brie, it reaped great rivers of wheat, which it shipped to the big mills in Paris to make flour, and mountains of sugar, which was then sold to wholesalers.

At harvest times, the seasonal laborers arrived at the farms by the hundreds, to thin, hoe, pull the sugar beets, reap, gather, and thresh the wheat. The company was very old, since, before us, my parents—and, I believe, my grandparents—had worked for it. Its profits were enormous: entire families of stockholders lived comfortably on their dividends in Paris, going to the central offices each month to collect their returns.

I was surprised by these revelations. In the almost thirty years that I had come to the farm, this was the first time I heard so much about the company at one swoop. My father had never asked any questions about his employers either. He was content to pocket his pay each season, so long as it was the right amount. And we had done the same. What stuck in my mind, though, was that there was a farm in Mitry, which was where my son was. This news hadn't fallen on deaf ears.

The months passed, and my husband and I worried more
and more about Auguste, who wrote us regularly. The cobbler
was going on three sprees a day, and his shop was neglected,
black, filthy. He was losing all his customers.

I didn't know how to get Auguste, my husband, to decide to
move to Mitry. I didn't dare ask him. And then one evening,
on his return from work, he brusquely asked me the question:
"Say, Marie-Cat, would it bother you a lot if we left Avay to
go to the Seine-et-Marne?" Then I realized that he, like me,
hadn't dared to ask. We were both dying to go, but neither
one had told the other.

It was easily arranged; the agent of the Avay refinery and
the Saint-Martin farm helped us. He wrote to Paris, and we
waited for an answer. It came a week later. The company
accepted our request to move—at our expense—to Mitry.
My husband would be employed at the refinery and I at the
farm. At busy times, Auguste was to return to the fields as a
wagon driver. We were assigned lodgings near the sugar-beet
refinery.   .

We moved in January 1931. We had said farewell to our
friends and acquaintances: the agent, his wife, the servants,
and several sugar workers. It was quickly done. In our life of
hard work, we had little time to build friendships. We didn't
need them anyway. We weren't talkative, especially Auguste;
he said that he had nothing to say to the others. When we
came home, it was to go to sleep, not to give parties.

We left Avay one fine morning for the Dieppe railroad
station. Our furniture had gone by train the day before. I went
around the house one last time, using a candle that I put in my
bag afterward, to make sure we hadn't forgotten anything. All
that was left was the bed frame lent us by the farm, on which
we had slept. I was upset to leave my home behind, but not as
much as when we left the cottage in Avesnes. I was so happy
at the thought of seeing my son again! We gave a last glance

at the church, whose bulk was becoming visible in the dawn, and hop! were on the road. Our valises were carried in one of the farm's wagons, which took us to the train.

We took the métro in Paris from the Gare Saint-Lazare to the Gare de l'Est. What a trip! We had never been on the subway before and didn't know how to take it to go from one place to another. Shaken, jostled, following directions given on the run by men rushing by, we ended up just the same at the station where we had to take the train to Meaux.

We got on it half an hour early in order to have time to get settled, and, while waiting for the departure, we watched the bustle at the railroad station with amazement. Each time a train pulled by us, it enveloped us in a cloud of steam; we were dumbfounded by the number of travelers getting off.

Auguste and I were curious and a little worried about the unknown awaiting us. The train pulled out slowly. We watched the landscape that went by with wide eyes. How forlorn it was! Enormous buildings hid the sky on both sides of the tracks. Laundry flapped in the wind outside the windows of apartment houses. Then came the factories in the suburbs. Suddenly I noticed something and grabbed Auguste's arm. On some huge warehouses I read GRANDS MOULINS DE PARIS. So it was there that the wheat ended up, the wheat both of us had harvested for years, and our parents before us. That unexpected sight gave us a jolt.

Little by little, the houses shrank in height. As the steam engine, panting like a tired animal, pulled us farther, settlement became more sparse, and it wasn't long before we saw the plains of Brie stretching off to the horizon. The brightness hurt our eyes that day because it had snowed for several hours and everything was white. It was a pure white, not yet dirtied by earth or soot.

In the compartment, it was hot enough to kill us, and we were eager to get to our destination. We still had to wait for the bus that was to take us to Mitry. The driver wasn't in a very good mood, what with the roads covered with snow. We made our way slowly through the countryside, which was very flat and uniform under the thick white blanket that covered it.

Finally, in the frozen, silent whiteness, we saw a steeple and some houses. It was Mitry, the town where we were going to live. We were dropped off in the square by the town hall, where a delivery truck was waiting., It was a favor from Mr. Hiet, the agent, who had sent someone to fetch us. We were very pleased.

The driver right away began to speak very familiarly to Auguste, which offended my husband a little.[1] He quickly got used to it. We were now in the Parisian region, and the customs were different than in Normandy. There was much less politeness toward neighbors or fellow workers. I felt right away that the world where we would live from then on was very different.

The driver of the truck was a thirsty character. He invited us to have a drink with him in a neighboring bar. He took a glass of red wine and was a little ticked off when Auguste ordered coffee. Then he told us some of what was ahead for us, especially the working conditions. "It's a forced-labor camp here. Not even a minute to go piss. The boss is always at your heels, spying on you." Auguste didn't say anything. He just listened. "The agent is looking forward to having you, Santerre. He says that you work hard. So much the better, you can give yourself with an open heart," the driver ended sarcastically.

We got back into the delivery truck. It wasn't much farther. The sugar refinery was near the barns, long brick buildings that were sprinkled with snow that day. Towering above it all, there was a very tall chimney. Around the chimney were fields, nothing but fields, but in the center of the scene were grouped the farm buildings. All of it was gloomy and ugly, and I felt my heart sink.

In the big courtyard, the piston of a steam engine drove up

and down regularly. I had to get used to that slow noise, like a giant ticking clock. During the busy season, when the sugar distilling was done, the piston's pulse marked the hours for the community that lived around it.

We were shown our lodgings, where our furniture and baskets had already been delivered. There were two rooms and a kitchen, and all our things had been dumped in the back room. Auguste didn't know where to start to arrange our furniture. First of all, however, we had to go meet Mr. Hiet.

We waited a few minutes and then he received us, very kindly, in a narrow office that smelled of musty paper. The office walls, like everything else, shook regularly from the repeated thrusts of the steam engine's piston. Mr. Hiet was very tall, broad-shouldered, and confident. He was also very cordial: "My colleague in Avay had the highest praise for both of you. I hope he didn't lie. I need people like you here. And now, go get settled in."

That's what we were doing that evening when the door opened. It was our son. What joy to see him again, taller but not much heavier! I immediately asked him to live with us. We would buy him a bed and armoire. He accepted without hesitation. He had had more than enough of his cousins. My husband and I were happy to have him with us again, to hug him and do things for him. He was with us at last, smiling as usual, a good boy, as he was all his life.

The very next day, I went to the farmhouse, to Mrs. Hiet, who directed the servants. At first, she seemed less friendly than my former boss, quieter, prouder. But it was only an impression, and I soon grew to appreciate her also. She was fine as long as one wasn't lazy, for she wasn't generous with sympathy. I didn't lack courage; I had had plenty since my childhood, and I didn't find the work there more unpleasant than my former job. Quite the contrary, it seemed better.

Auguste was of the same opinion. He was put in charge of the horses, which he found poorly cared for, uncurried, living in filthy straw. Auguste was very fond of horses, and he respected them. He said that they were fellow workers, true comrades who never shirked their work. He never used a whip because he understood horses. A whip was unnecessary, for when the horse got used to its task, it went practically on its own, as a reasonable animal that knew it must work every day.

Auguste was soon the friend of the four Percherons that lived together in one large stable. He began with a complete wash of the brick floor with chlorine. Then he whitewashed the walls and curried the powerful bodies at length, braiding their manes and tails. Mr. Hiet, who went to the stable the next day, said not a word. But in the next fifteen years, my husband never saw him there again. The animals had everything they needed, unstinting portions of oats and hay. Auguste was generous to the horses. "They can't ask for anything. We have a tongue, we can defend ourselves, but they . . ." he said to his friends, who laughingly accused him of pampering his Percherons.

So our life at Mitry fell into a routine. We had the same schedules, the same duties as in Normandy. In the morning, I went to the farm and Auguste to the refinery. And we met again each evening with our son, discussing the day that was ending and the one tomorrow.

But I had a hard time getting used to our new lodgings. They were gloomy and always noisy, with the pounding of the steam engine resonating in our ears day and night. In addition, when it was sugar-beet–harvest time, trucks were forever driving in and out with their loads of beets. The beets followed a precise schedule, from the entry dock to the washing vats. It was at the scales, where they were weighed, that the hubbub and bustle were greatest. Then came the noise of the conveyor, followed by the rush of the roots sliding into the iron vats where they were shaken clear of dirt. Trucks were constantly being driven up to the building; we could also hear teams of horses that came from close by.

To all that was added the shipment of the pulp. That was what was left of the beets after their treatment at the refinery. The pulp was sold as cattle feed. It was a sort of yellowish purée that spattered all over the floor and made people slip. The pulp was shipped out in big freight cars which were pulled down a railroad siding owned by the company. The Mitry railroad station came to life in an uninterrupted concert of locomotive whistles when the pulp was ready to be shipped. The powerful smell of pulp penetrated everywhere. Even our bedsheets were impregnated with it.

During the busy season at the refinery, Auguste alternated shifts: one week of days, from 7:00 to 9:00, and one week of nights, from 7:00 to 7:00. Outside the factory there was continuous activity. The convoys of trucks arrived, leaving oceans of sugar beets, covered with mud; when they left, the trucks were often loaded with pulp. The piston on the big copper boiler beat the rhythm for this coming and going. Its wheel, as tall as two men, furnished the motor power for the conveyor belts and machines.

At dawn, I was never eager to go to work at the neighboring farm. There, things were awful. The farm laborers were dissatisfied, and French seasonal workers became rare. They said that they no longer wanted to do "starvation work."

Instead of French workers at the wheat and sugar-beet harvests, there were Belgians, and silent, strong Poles who had to follow sign language, as they didn't understand French.

One day, my boss told me that the farm had been sold. Discouraged by the problems of agriculture, the company had sold it to a neighboring farmer. I didn't like that man, who was brutal and bossy. His wife wasn't much nicer. Soon after they moved in, I had a curious experience there that led to my quitting.

I was cleaning their room and lifted a carpet. Under it I found a five-hundred-franc bill. I hesitated over what to do. Should I give it to them or leave it where it was? I finally

chose the second solution. But that discovery made me uneasy. Auguste said it was surely a test of my honesty. I was
scandalized by such goings-on. Since they didn't even trust
me, I thought it was useless to stay on, and I quit.

For a while, I did seasonal work again with the Belgians and
Poles, working for other farmers in Mitry. But I was alone,
without Auguste, in the midst of all those strangers. I was
unhappy, unable to speak a word to anyone around me. They
all lived in terror of being fired if they didn't work hard
enough. So they stayed bent over the earth for hours and
hours, not daring to so much as raise their heads. To top it all,
in the evening when we returned from the fields, we were
often insulted by the French workers at the neighboring brickworks, who were waiting to taunt us as we passed and to throw
clods of dirt at us, yelling that we were scabs.

For the first time in my life, I chickened out. I couldn't do it
any longer. I didn't understand what was going on around me
or what all the agitation was about.

Auguste, at the refinery, noticed the same thing. Everything was in limbo there, too. Sometimes, the workers
gathered together to protest. They thought that the boss was
unfair when he refused to raise their salaries.

Production lost its beautiful regularity. My husband and I
were surprised at this whole protest movement. From childhood, we had worked without question, from dawn to night,
like our parents, our brothers, our cousins. The thought of
protesting against our working conditions never occurred to
us. Now everything had changed. From then on, the big silent
group that we were part of resisted their employers. The
bosses, in turn, hired foreign laborers to replace those who
quit with muttered warnings of revolution.

One evening, when we were getting ready to go to bed,
someone knocked at the door. The man there said that he
belonged to the union. He was friendly and spoke persua-
sively. He asked us to join the union to protect ourselves.

Auguste refused, saying that he was big enough to take care of himself. They argued together. "Don't you understand, Santerre, that you are being exploited?" said the man. "Why don't you have Sunday to rest a little, or vacations either? And your salary? How much do you and your wife earn? Will you tell me?"

I realized that, all in all, we didn't make much. For twenty-seven years, my husband and I had never ceased working, and we had put only a couple of hundred francs aside. We talked about it in bed, and he too, although still as reasonable as ever, ended by agreeing that we were being abused.

One day, when I went to the grocery store in Mitry, I heard a rumpus in the streets. The noise was still far off, but when I left the store, I noticed people listening curiously in their doorways. And suddenly, around a corner not far from the church, a group of men and women marched, carrying signs. Someone said that they were the workers from the brickworks and the foundry. For the first time in my life I heard those words that the mass of people on the road were shouting: "On strike! On strike! On strike!"

The words came at me full blast, expelled from hundreds of chests. The crowd continued to the refinery. I followed it because I was going in that direction also. It halted before the huge door, its members continuing to shout. Suddenly the strikers changed their slogan, yelling at the top of their lungs: "Join us! Join us!"

The noise was so great that it drowned out the pounding of the steam engine. The men from the refinery came out to look and then joined those in the road. Some cheered. People poured from the buildings, attracted by the yelling. Soon everyone was outside, gesticulating and arguing, while the boiler piston continued its rhythmic beat. That lasted several minutes. Suddenly the raucous whistle of the refinery, reverberating mournfully, called the workers to their morning work. A jet of steam escaped from the big beveled metal tube of the factory whistle.

It was like a signal. The sugar workers all returned to the buildings while the crowd resumed its march toward the farm. As the strikers left, some threw stones at the front windows of the refinery and the glass broke with a crash.

On the days that followed, the same scene was repeated. Crowds of strikers wandered the streets of Mitry and even went into the countryside, where they frightened the farm workers. In the brickworks, the fires in the kilns that had burned for years went out. The crucible at the foundry, which had burned day and night, was also extinguished. Workers walked out of shops and factories everywhere to join the strike.

It was a Tuesday when the refinery shut down. I was at home, in my kitchen, since, for several weeks, Auguste hadn't wanted me to go to the fields. Suddenly there was silence. I wondered what could have happened; something was missing. I gradually understood what made me uneasy: it was the silence, an absolute, complete silence. The steam engine had stopped. It was extraordinary. I realized at that moment to what extent the steam boiler had become part of our lives, all day and all night, every day and every night. The walls stopped shaking, and the pans in the cupboard no longer vibrated with the never-ending clinking sound that accompanied all my hours as a housewife.

The whistle of the refinery began to sound shrilly. All the steam accumulated by the engine escaped through the siren, in huge clouds, released by the stoker, who no doubt feared an explosion. You could hear its long wail all through Mitry. The life of the sugar-beet factory escaped through the whistle in a long breath, like the siren of a boat in distress, about to sink. In the buildings, the distilling apparatus with its long iron sleeves, the vats with their steel hooks, the conveyor belt scaffolding as tall as a house, the hoppers still full of beets—all stopped dead. The little engines that pulled the metal wagons full of pulp also let off steam, released by the mechanics, who were abandoning them where they were. The high-pitched whistle of those engines was the final protest of the suddenly silent mass of bricks. The strike at the refinery had begun!

Chapter Eight

Auguste joined the strike. I didn't go back to work either. The union puffed up the workers' hopes and predicted confidently that the great day had come. The great day, that is, when our lives would improve. I never believed it, but Auguste swallowed it all. He thought things had to change. He said that we would have vacations, adequate salaries. I didn't believe it, but still I didn't argue. For me, my husband was always right. And from the moment he decided something, it was inevitably good.

On the first day of the work stoppage, Auguste met with the agent. Their conversation was short but lively. "So, even you, Santerre," said Mr. Hiet, who looked very pale and tired. "Even you are letting me down." "Yes, monsieur, I am letting you down, as you say. Because I'm fed up! Fed up with this rotten life, work without a stop, without rest, without anything. Mr. Hiet, we are not animals!" my husband replied.

It seemed to him that Mr. Hiet smiled a little, and that made him angrier. My poor Auguste, who never got angry, became violently so. "No, not animals! Furthermore, your cattle are better cared for than we are. And I know the reason.

Well, that's all finished! I want to rest on Sunday without having to lose two hours of pay to go to mass, and that only with your permission. And, Mr. Hiet, from time to time, I would like to see something besides fields, always fields. I was born in 1889, and since my childhood I have seen only fields. Worse still, I look only at the ground; I've never had the time to lift my eyes and enjoy the countryside. So, you see, I would like a change. Now, I must also tell you: if I happen to have two hundred francs put aside, it's because my wife and I have worked hard and long. Otherwise, we'd be like many others, without a sou, without even the right to get sick."

Auguste finally stopped, dumbfounded to have said so much at one time. The two men parted, both sad and both regretting having come to such hard words.

The third day of the strike we received a letter from the company. It informed us, very curtly, that if we hadn't gone back to work in a week, we would be fired.

Groups gathered to talk in the village. No one knew what to do. The fathers with large families wanted to go back to work. At home, the wives worried. We were living as well as we could on our savings and with the help the unions gave to the worst off. But if, to top it off, we were to lose our jobs, it would be impossible.

Ten days after the beginning of the work stoppage, almost all the workers were there at the gate, heads bowed like beaten dogs. In the courtyard there were police, and a whole squadron of troops in steel helmets, brought by truck from Paris. They guarded the plant with guns at the ready. The sugar workers went back to work again, with the same wages. But not for long. It was election time, and a new government was elected.

My husband and I had never voted. But the mayor of Mitry, a Socialist who had just recently been elected, came to see us. He persuaded us that we had to vote that time. We registered at the town hall. We put the ballot for the candidate with three red arrows on his posters into the voting urn, and he was elected our deputy.[1] This awesome man had passed through Mitry once; he visited the town hall and went through the streets, into the factories, to incite the workers to continue their struggle. At the brickworks and the foundry, the strike had lasted longer than ours, and people said that they had obtained improvements.

When the Blum government came in, matters improved quickly. My husband said that the company people in Paris had been forced to bend over backward. There were fierce disagreements between the unions and the bosses. The bosses, accustomed as they had been for centuries to having their way, had to give in to the angry men in shirtsleeves who sat across the table from them. The workers wouldn't let them continue the same old ways.

People said that the director-general of the company—the son of the one I had seen in Avay—was treated roughly in the negotiations. The delegates from the Nord, the Seine-Inférieure, and the Seine-et-Marne brusquely presented him with their four demands, without formality. We later received a pamphlet in which the interview was described.

The unions had begun by comparing the company's capital and its rising profits. The millions harvested by the seasonal laborers flowed to the central office, a big carved-stone building on one of the boulevards of Paris. The workers' delegates bluntly pointed out the continuing injustice of company policy and its exploitation of the poor. It hired temporary workers for the season, with no job security, and laid them off as soon as the earth had given its wheat or sugar beets, sending them back to their misery. The company was not concerned about what became of them and it did not hire them back until the next year, after a layoff of five or six months, during which they could have starved.

The director-general, in a cold voice, then explained that the company had supported hundreds of families who were well content to have found that work. After all, they were free not to work, but if they did work, they were lodged and fed.

Then the discussion became truly ugly. The delegates from the Seine-et-Marne, above all, were fierce. Many were the sons of seasonal laborers who remembered the long days their parents had worked. They were men who still had the taste in their mouths of the vegetable soup distributed by the ladleful at the farms. They vented their indignation, their anger at all the accumulated miseries, the diseases that couldn't be cured, the helpless old people who died—all for lack of money.

Finally, they thrust a worker-protection plan under the noses of the bosses' delegation. Seasonal labor would be abolished, and all agricultural workers would get contracts. Later, we got social-security cards. The company representatives didn't have any choice. They had to give in to the threat of nationalization that the men in shirtsleeves brought up again and again.

I had no strong opinion about all this. I wasn't angry at the company people, who had never harmed me. My parents and Auguste and I had always had a good relationship with them. At the same time, I felt strongly that we were repaying age-old injustices, which we had accepted without question because we didn't understand. Everything was changing so quickly now that one could hardly keep up.

From that time on, we were off on Sundays. My husband and I had a hard time getting used to it, but we liked it fine. During the sugar-refining season, Auguste still worked on holidays, but he got paid double, so he had no complaints.

After the strike, Mr. Hiet, the agent, never scolded my husband for what he had said in their discussion. Anyway, he too should have been happy, since he didn't have to work on Sundays anymore either.

One day, he offered us a change in housing. There was an apartment available, away from the refinery, on the road to the railroad station, in some houses owned by the company. We accepted without hesitation. I didn't like where we were. It was small, and the noise from the engine was unpleasant. Then there was the smell of pulp, which penetrated everywhere, so strongly that we felt as though we were eating it at meals.

The place we moved into reminded me a little of my childhood *coron*. Running from the refinery to the railroad station, there was a row of brick houses, all the same, bordering the road. Some were a bit larger than the others: those were reserved for the supervisors. All the houses had gardens. A flowering hedge separated us from our neighbors. But the poor bushes were so thin that they didn't hide anything that happened on the other side.

During that period, I didn't go out to work, but the time wore on me, with nothing to do. So I began working days at another farm in Mitry. I took care of the kitchen and cleaning. The work wasn't heavy, and it was well paid. The farm owners were nice, and the staff was treated with respect. I began at 8:00 in the morning and finished at 6:00 P.M. For me, it was like living in a château, with such short workdays!

Soon after this, the troubles of my son and his boss began. Two new barbers had set up in the town, and there was stiff competition. Little by little, the customers thinned out and Auguste began to work only half-days. He was very worried, poor fellow. One day, he announced that he had found another job to compensate for the drop in his earnings. He had signed up at the brick factory, as a laborer loading trucks. His father would have preferred that Auguste work with him at the refinery. But Auguste didn't like the dark buildings, and he couldn't stand the smell of pulp. I could understand that, for he had worked all day in a salon that smelled of eau de cologne!

So he worked at the brick factory from 6:00 in the morning

until noon. Finally, the barber, discouraged, closed his shop. He was on the verge of going broke. He would have had to modernize his shop, but he didn't have the money, and his two competitors were well set up.

Auguste, my husband, whom I had begun to call "Pépé," to differentiate him from the other, was mulling over a project and, one evening, he told us about it. In Mitry, there was a woman who was originally from the same village as us in the Nord. She ran a café near the town hall. I saw her there sometimes when I was running errands in town. She and Auguste arranged that she would rent my son a room next to the bar. Equipping himself with a rotating chair and a table with a mirror sold to him by his former boss, my son set up on his own. He was open only on Saturday and Sunday. The rest of the week, he worked full-time at the brickworks. He did very well. Many clients liked him a lot and came back to be barbered by him, especially since his two days were very convenient, at the end of the week. As for the owner of the café, she was very pleased. The two businesses each promoted the other. The clients, while waiting for their turn, drank a bit, and they only had to go to the next room to be barbered.

And if that could have kept up, my God, there wouldn't have been any complaints. Our life was good, and we didn't have any money worries. Oh, we weren't earning hundreds and thousands, but we were happy. At the refinery, Pépé still took care of the horses, which the company kept even though there were tractors which were faster and more powerful for pulling the mechanical harvesters through the fields.

Then one day—it was when people had begun to talk of war again—I was preparing the noon meal at the farm. It was boiled beef, I remember. I was humming the song that poor Paul had liked so much:

If you think I will tell you
Whom I dare to admire . . .

118

My song was interrupted by shouts outside the kitchen: "Madame Santerre, Madame Santerre!" I ran to the back doorstep anxiously. A man covered from head to foot with a fine red dust waved his arms. "Come quickly, Madame Santerre. Your son has had an accident!"

What accident? I didn't understand. The man, a worker from the brickworks, explained to me that, while loading a truck, Auguste had been hit by an armful of six bricks that his predecessor in the chain had passed on too soon, before he had turned around. That was how they usually moved the bricks, passing them from one man to another, from the storehouse to the truck. Most of the time, it worked well. The armfuls landed safely in the big leather gloves and were passed to the neighbor right away. This time, the chain had "broken." The worst was that Auguste was at the bottom of the line, so the bricks had dropped on him from several meters above.

I left at a run. At our house, I found my son spread out on his bed. Three workers were sponging his head. Under his beret, red with brick dust, blood made a darker stain. Soon after, the doctor arrived. He examined Auguste's skull carefully, cutting off the stickiest hair. "All right. . . . This doesn't look so bad. Set your mind at ease, madame," he told me. "There is nothing broken." He carefully cleaned the wound and put on a dressing.

He came back each day for a week. Auguste quickly recovered, and we were reassured. He kept his bandage on for ten days; then he only had some sticking plaster, which he covered with the beret that he wore all the time. He went back to work, and the months passed.

Meanwhile, he got married and went to live with his wife in Mitry. Our hearts were heavy to see him go. But that was life. What I had done, he did in turn; it was normal. I thought back to how my parents must have felt when I left them. And I wasn't an only daughter. One had to get used to it, as one has to get used to everything, to the good and bad things that came, one after the other, in our poor lives. We had little choice. Events were imposed on us; we had to accept the consequences. Nevertheless, I never liked my daughter-in-law.

We soon had other reasons for worry. People around us talked more and more of war. At the farm, my boss was anxious. After a respite, during which we thought the danger had passed, unpleasant rumors began to circulate again, persistently.

Pépé didn't believe it would all really begin again. We were just getting on our feet after the last one; it was unrealistic to believe that there would be another war. Others said the opposite. Still others were for giving the Boches a good licking. It would be a question of days, quickly over. The Germans wouldn't have the time to draw a deep breath. Me, I listened to these men and found them a little optimistic. They had an excuse for letting their heads swell, with all the baloney that was circulating at the time. The newspapers and the radio never ceased declaring that we were the strongest, the greatest. But Auguste and I, as we didn't read the one or listen to the other, were less deceived by the foolish propaganda which gave people false hopes. We were suspicious. We remembered how, in 1914, we had been caught by surprise in Normandy.

"What if it starts again like the last one?" Auguste asked his friends. But they said he was a defeatist, a fool. Besides, what did he know of war, he who had never fought?

War was declared on Germany in a climate of optimism. The men called to their country's flag probably weren't that happy to go, but they believed that it wouldn't be long before they would have the enemy on his knees, begging for mercy. My son had been rejected when he was called up for military service, like his father twenty years before. He had flat feet. At the mobilization, he went to Paris anyway, to the post at Clignancourt, for a physical exam. The major confirmed his exemption; he also told Auguste to watch out for his left arm, which had bad reflexes. For some time, he had had problems on some days, during which, it seemed to him, his arm was partially paralyzed, making it difficult to cut hair.

Business at the barbershop thinned out. Most of the men were gone, and we had the same difficulties as in 1914. It was the same at the refinery and the farm. But the problem of lack of workers was less serious, because this time there were machines to substitute.

We settled into a curious state, in a war that wasn't really a war. Pépé brought home comforting news every evening, armfuls of victories on all fronts. Still, I saw that we weren't advancing much for all that. My husband answered that, with the Maginot Line, we didn't need to. As for the neighborhood women, whose husbands were at the front, they received letters about playing cards, about listening to the radio under the stars, about the distribution of hot wine.

There were occasional sour notes. A refinery worker died, killed in isolated combat. He was the father of three children and, apparently, he wasn't playing cards. Italy's entry into the war triggered snickering in the town: "With the Macaronis, it's always the same. Just like in 1914. Always trying to jump ahead in the game."

Then, in one swift moment, the comedy turned to tragedy. We were caught out in the cold just like that, dumbly, without expecting it. Holland, then Belgium were invaded and, after them, France. My little village of Avesnes, in the Nord, was once again being overrun.

Even though Pépé still brought home news of military successes every day, he reported them with less and less conviction. The first refugees arrived from the east. They moved into the refinery building, which was silent and empty at that time of the year. Many took refuge there. First came trucks and automobiles, which could move the most rapidly. Then came the horse-drawn wagons, carrying crowds of people, furniture, and clothes, with cows tethered behind. Then there were the pitiful pedestrians, the poor people who fled with handcarts, wheelbarrows, baby carriages, carrying what they could with them.

We watched them sympathetically, not suspecting that our turn was next, and sooner than we could believe. Auguste, reporting the news he heard at the refinery, spoke of a temporary withdrawal. There was no doubt: we were on the verge of victory! The Germans had only a couple of liters of gas, and people said that their tanks were pulled by horses!

One morning we began to see soldiers, many soldiers—too many soldiers. That didn't mean anything good. It was our turn to hear the alarm, the horrible cry of war: "The Germans are coming! They are at Château-Thierry!"

It was my boss, the farmer, who helped us escape one evening around 5:00. We drove off with a tractor and a trailer, in which we put some baggage, but not much, to avoid weighing it down. He released his animals into the fields, for fear that they would slow our flight. Pépé and I were perched on a mattress. The boss and his wife sat in front on the tractor, which he drove.

First he tried to go to Paris. But he had to give that up. That was where everyone was desperately heading, hoping to put themselves within the shelter of the walls of a big city. It was almost like an animal instinct. There was a frightful traffic jam, so we bore to the left to go toward Melun. In the Brie countryside, there was confused traffic in all directions. Cars, bikes, motorcycles, buses, wagons, handcarts—anything that would move was fleeing south. At Melun, we had a close call. The army engineers were going to blow up the bridge, and the officers said our way would be cut off. We couldn't go very far anyway in the mess ahead of us, they said.

Here we had some luck. My boss knew the officer slightly. He was a notary from the Seine-et-Marne. So he let us pass with a big wave of his arm. At Nemours, the commotion was frightening. Some military convoys were going toward the front, others were retreating; all were entangled in a dreadful mess. Officers—helmeted, with pistols drawn—cleared the way with threats, forcing the vehicles of the refugees onto the shoulders of the roads. Some cavalry officers actually cut the harnesses of farm wagons with their sabers to prevent their going any farther.

We got through as well as could be expected. My boss headed toward Nevers, but by such a circular route that we hardly made any forward progress. He stayed clear of the major roads, where frightened people stretched to the horizons. In the evening, we looked for a wood in which to spend the night. We slept on the trailer or spread out on the mattress. Luckily, the weather was very mild. My boss had plenty of gas. He had three enormous cans of it that he hid under the baggage in the trailer. Many refugees didn't have enough gas and were ready to do anything to get some, prowling in the dark, like murderers, wild with the fear of being stuck in the middle of the country, at the mercy of the invading Germans.

I don't know how we succeeded in getting to Montargis. We arrived in the evening, around 6:00, in an extraordinary traffic jam. The news was more and more alarming. The Germans were literally at our backs.

It was a beautiful day, very warm, and we were at the gates of the city, blocked by immense crowds of people, when we suddenly heard airplanes. Each time the motors buzzed by in the sky, panic seized the refugees, who abandoned their vehicles to throw themselves in the ditch. Sirens wailed as the sinister birds dove at us, spraying machine-gun fire up and down the road, sweeping the traffic and setting cars on fire by exploding their gas tanks. Fear-crazed horses bolted and ran, the wagons they dragged contributing to the disaster as they crushed everything in their way. There were also the dead, and the injured calling for help from where they lay. No one helped them; everyone was preoccupied solely with his own life.

Later that day, when the buzz of the propellers sounded again above our heads, there was a brief panic. Then people yelled, "Don't be scared, those are French . . . those are French!"

So, reassured, we waved in friendship. We could practically see the flags, which were definitely different from the familiar, awful black swastikas. Suddenly, those airplanes that we had believed were ours poured forth iron and fire, again slaughtering the trusting civilians. It was horrible: people cut down in the midst of gaiety, when for once they weren't hiding themselves. The four of us slid quickly under the trailer. That saved our lives.

Suddenly my boss, whose face was streaming with sweat, yelled, "Name of God, name of God! Those are Italians!"

Again we heard groans, cries of pain. Military trucks passed, but fewer and fewer of them. Fleeing tanks had pitilessly pushed cars to the side of the road, where they burned in big clouds of thick smoke. My boss was lucky enough to receive permission to hide our tractor in a neighboring farmyard. Fire spread all along the pitiful convoy as everyone abandoned it, fleeing toward the center of the city.

In the midst of this awful mess, we heard a little later the regular noise of motors and the sound of guttural voices, curtly giving orders. We waited in the deserted farmyard. Suddenly, tall blond soldiers burst in, dressed in spotted uniforms, machine guns in their arms. They ignored us, running to the buildings, where they kicked open the doors before sweeping the farm and its cellar with waves of bullets to clear out any opposition. We were half-dead with fear. It all happened so quickly. Then a soldier arrived in an armored car and came toward us. His face was black with oil and dust except where his goggles, pushed up into his hair, had left a white mark. He stopped close to us. He was armed with an enormous revolver. We thought our last minute had come. I began to pray.

This man, in helmet and leather boots, was surrounded by other soldiers like himself, all armed to the teeth. I remember clearly what he said, in unaccented French: "Have no fear, ladies! We aren't barbarians, we don't kill civilians."

So it was that our exodus ended.

Several days later, our group, provided with a pass, turned around and went back to Mitry, where an unhappy period awaited us.

Chapter Nine

~~~ · ~~~

We finally reached our home after many difficulties. There was real chaos all along the roads: burned military vehicles, destroyed houses, and ruined bridges. We had to form long lines and borrow boats to get across the rivers. Everywhere we went, the Germans were settling in, and many official buildings were already flying the red flags with black swastikas on white backgrounds. As we left Melun, there was a distressing scene between my boss and an officer in a black uniform who commanded the post. He bluntly refused us access to the highway and directed us to a small road across the plain that went God knows where.

The farmer equally bluntly refused to go that way with the tractor and trailer, persisting in wanting to go to the right. It was awful. The officer, a tall, red-faced blond, drew his revolver and yelled threats in German, brandishing the weapon under our noses and saying in very correct French that he would kill us all. *

---

*The impasse was ended by the arrival of high-ranking officers who allowed the group to pass.—Trans.

When we arrived at our house, a very unpleasant surprise awaited us. The door was hanging open, and our belongings were all gone. No more linen, no more dishes, nothing! Looters had passed through. Pépé and I cried. Once again, thirty years after the first time, we had lost everything. We had only the few clothes we had taken with us. In the basement there remained a keg of beer and some forty kilos of sugar which my husband had bought shortly before our departure. As we had fled, he had balanced a long board on the stairs, which probably hindered the thieves.

Auguste decided to go see Mr. Hiet. But in the courtyard of the refinery, he stopped in shock. It was full of dark green cars, and at the doorway a sentinel was guarding the entry. The agent was in his office, but he was pale and weary-looking. He told my husband that the army was requisitioning the refinery, which would work for the occupiers from then on. The new head was to be a fat old officer. "A Bavarian farmer," said Mr. Hiet. "As for me, I'm nothing anymore, I have no authority. We all have to obey him now."

The officer was a terror in his khaki uniform.[1] He never put down his leather whip, with which he constantly tapped his boots. The workers were scared stiff. He started off right away by attacking a driver with his whip, when the man refused to take off his hat to him. The whip whistled many times, slashing the face of the poor guy until he begged pardon on his knees. The soldiers, mostly old men, stood around watching this violent scene silently.

Thus Captain Schmidt took over at the refinery. In no time, he was hated by one and all. I couldn't stand him. Even the sight of him made me sick, with his satisfied air and his habit of straightening himself while walking, pulling his tunic down in back, and tapping his boots. Auguste received a pass to come and go into the refinery with his horses and take them into the fields. Like all his friends, he never forgot to remove his hat when the "Hauptmann" passed him, stiff and conceited.

Our son returned several days after us. He had fled by train to Châteauroux with his wife's parents. When he came to see us, he complained about his arm, which bothered him more and more. It was becoming difficult for him to move it. My husband advised him to go see a doctor, who examined him carefully. That was when we learned that the paralysis was probably the result of his head injury.

He never was able to reopen his salon. The brickworks took him on as a checker, but he didn't earn much and times were hard. From then on, there were many shortages in France, in the war years and after.

Pépé and I suffered little, having been accustomed for a long time to ration ourselves. We had to forget meat again, of course, which we had begun to enjoy eating. With our garden and the few rabbits and chickens my husband raised, we hung on. I sometimes brought home a little butter or some potatoes from the farm. The worst was coffee. We had to line up for hours to get a package, which tasted like dirt, worse than the chicory of my childhood. As for fuel, to the stupefaction of our neighbors, my husband made it himself. He had obtained authorization from Captain Schmidt to collect the coal-dust scrapings from the floor of the boiler room—permission that the officer gave with a snicker, muttering in German. To this blackish dust, Pépé added a sort of glaze, found around the brickworks, and he formed it all into little balls. From the first try, it was successful. It gave off a dreadful odor, but it burned and it heated. Pépé, smiling, said that the training in making briquettes in Avesnes had been useful to us after all.

Others wanted to profit from the surplus coal dust too. But when they came to ask permission, the Hauptmann sent them off without an explanation, lashing his boots harder than ever with his whip. I don't know why he refused others what he allowed my husband to do, but I believe that he appreciated the care Auguste gave to the horses. Often, he himself went to the stable to caress their silky skins. He was very fond of them.

Maybe they reminded him of his own horses, left behind on his farm in Bavaria. When he rubbed the backs of the Percherons, a glimmer of tenderness passed through his eyes. One day, he gave a present to Auguste. He took off his jacket and demonstrated. With the equipment he brought and a little bottle that came with a brush, he drew little squares and diamonds on the rumps of the horses, which looked as if they were printed on the hair. He stepped back, pleased with himself. "We do that to horses in Germany," he declared, satisfied.

Auguste took that as an order, and he too learned to print on the rumps of the Percherons. And the fat captain didn't miss a chance, when he met Auguste with a team, to examine the beasts. Then he would murmur, "*Gut . . . gut . . . Schön . . . schön . . .*"

This shared love of horses was useful to Pépé several times when he was given little bottles of sugar syrup. Although they made it all day long, the workers were forbidden to take sugar, under threat of severe punishment. So we had to be content with the meager ration from the grocery store, bought at the beginning of each month. The sugar syrup was used for making the designs in the horses' short hair. My husband used as little as possible, bringing the rest of the bottle home.

We both went on with our work. I left each morning for the farm, at the same time as Auguste went to the factory for his job. We lived in the middle of German soldiers and ended by getting used to their presence. In the town, the flag with the swastika flew over the house of a Parisian factory owner—a Jew, people said. The house had been requisitioned, and the military headquarters, the Kommandatur, had moved in.

Amid all the difficulties of rationing that my husband and I endured, there was one thing whose loss we really felt. It was bread. From childhood on, bread had had great importance in my life. At the worst moments, there was always some in the house, some good white bread, with a golden crust that gave off a delicious odor of warm, well-risen dough. But the bread we got during the Occupation didn't resemble that at all. It was made of a sort of thick, viscous pulp. If we didn't eat it the day we got it, the next day it was impossible. It would be hard as rock and a yellowish color, strange and unhealthy.

My boss at the farm declared with a smile that it was truly bread from the other world. "Luckily," he added, "it won't last long. We'll see white bread again when those bastards have gone."

My boss was a patriot who didn't like the Germans at all. He didn't hide it either. And when he brought his crop to their cooperative, he was sick with anger on his return. His wife advised him to be careful, urging him to keep quiet. She was suspicious of some of the farm workers, one couple above all. They were Poles who were responsible for the stable, and their quick and cunning eyes were everywhere, peering into everything. I didn't like those two either. Several times when I was running errands in the town, I saw them in a café, talking with soldiers, for they spoke German very well. But my boss laughed at these worries and said that the Kuppas— those were the workers—were really good people and good workers.

We never suspected how that would end, so brutally, so tragically. It was a December morning, several days before my birthday. We were in the kitchen, busy preparing a meal, when a military vehicle pulled into the farm courtyard.

Four men got out, wearing turned-down hats and dressed in black leather. They entered without knocking and, speaking to the boss's wife, asked where her husband was. She pointed to the next room, the office where the farmer was doing his accounts. She wanted to call him. But with a sour smile, one of the men said no. They went into the room, closing the door behind them.

The boss's wife was white. We listened, worried. At first, we could only hear the sound of a voice, monotonous, mur-

muring. Then we heard blows, broken glass, overturned furniture, followed by a long, agonizing silence. Suddenly there were screams of pain—unbearable screams which froze the blood in our veins. The door of the office was brutally shoved open, and two of the Nazis dragged the farmer in. His face was bloody and his hands were covered with wounds. At the same moment, we smelled a horrible odor, an odor of burned flesh. Then I understood how he had been tortured. His two hands had been pressed and held on the top of the white-hot stove that heated the office! They took him out, poor man, and we never saw him again. After the Liberation, we learned that he had been deported to Germany and had died in a concentration camp.

His arrest caused an enormous stir. I was amazed to learn that my boss had been the head of a Resistance network and that he had surely been betrayed. It wasn't hard to figure out who did it. If one had any doubts, they didn't last long. Several days later, the Kuppas left the farm and took over a café near the Kommandatur. They bought the café from its proprietor, whose husband was a prisoner of war.

That café became a rendezvous for all the enemy soldiers, a collaborators' hangout. For weeks, I didn't leave my boss's wife. The poor woman was in terrible shape. What amazed me was her hair: it turned completely white in less than a week. She too had had to go to the Kommandatur, where she was interrogated. But she knew nothing of her husband's activities, so she was sent back to the farm. She died several years later, after the Liberation, dying of sorrow, no doubt.

The scene I had witnessed shook me profoundly. For the first time, I was exposed to human cruelty that was beyond imagination. For months, the sight of a black car passing by my door made me weak in the knees; I began to tremble, fearing that it was going to get Pépé at the refinery. I found out later who the men in the turned-down hats were: they were agents of the German secret police, the Gestapo. We sometimes saw them driving around the town. Several times they went to the refinery to question workers whom they later took away, just like my boss.

On those days, my husband returned to our house sick with fear. Even Captain Schmidt made himself as inconspicuous as possible when he saw the Gestapo. He went easy, smiling, giving orders in a calm voice.

One morning, outside the house, I heard a hubbub of screams and cars roaring past. Soldiers were running in the streets. A neighbor told me the news: Kuppa, the Pole, had been assassinated as he left his café, shot with a revolver.

To describe the following days would be impossible. Everywhere in the town, there were searches, interrogations, incarcerations. The mayor was imprisoned for a week. The day of Kuppa's funeral, everyone stayed inside. In the streets, the houses were silent and the shutters of the stores were closed. Armed soldiers escorted the hearse while the church bell tolled. Auguste stayed home and we spent a miserable day, each minute fearing the worst. There were many arrests in the town. Men were taken away at dawn and, like my boss, never seen again.

Although we didn't realize it, the hour of the Liberation was approaching. Our troubles weren't over yet, though. Each day, one could hear a distant rumble high in the sky of enormous airplanes passing above. We soon learned their name— Flying Fortresses. People said that they were going to drop their bombs on Germany. We congratulated ourselves that the bombs were not being dropped on us! But that didn't last long. After the Paris region was hit, it was our turn.

One morning I was working in the chicken yard of the farm when I saw planes overhead, flying lower than usual, which wasn't a good sign. I knew my husband was in the fields with his horses, spreading manure. Then I heard the siren start to shrill.

At the first sound of the siren, the factory whistle sounded too, causing panic everywhere. Everyone fled to the nearby dugout shelters over by the train station, while the big planes with tricolored emblems—it wasn't Italians that time—circled above. There were five, escorted by three smaller ones that skimmed along the ground and then climbed back into the sky with a frightening roar, no doubt to inform the others. Suddenly, all moving together, the bombers descended slowly, sighting on the target. Here and there, one could hear ridiculous bursts of machine-gun fire, directed at the attacking planes by the soldiers from the Kommandatur. Methodically, one after another, the airplanes passed over the refinery and the train station, each dropping a string of bombs, alternating explosive and incendiary ones, following a well-calculated plan. All hell broke loose, but it lasted only about five minutes. Those of us on the ground felt as though the minutes were hours.

The earth around the refinery looked as if it had been flung around by a giant hand; then the bombs plowed up the neighboring fields. The railroad station, whipped by the bombs, was pulverized by an avalanche of iron and fire, while the tracks were blown five hundred meters in the direction of the fields. The steel rails were twisted and broken like bits of wire.

Then it was the refinery's turn, targeted precisely by the airplanes so that the nearby houses, like ours, were barely damaged. The first bomb fell in the courtyard, where the explosion blew the heart out of the big steam engine, which was still going. The boiler burst and began to vomit white steam. The piston was flattened like a cookie, and the huge flywheel was torn loose and rolled twenty meters away, crunching partitions in its way with its five tons of momentum. Incendiary bombs rained down, exploding like firecrackers and spraying fire on the shattered beams. Next it was the turn of the storehouses, and a powerful odor of caramel spread for a kilometer around. Thousands of kilos of sugar in sacks were grilled in a shower of blue flames. Slowly, the last bomber arrived to finish the job. The tall brick chimney, miraculously, was still erect. The final bombs hit its base, where the furnace was, and it collapsed after swaying for a few seconds. It fell as if one mass: nothing remained but a pile of red dust several meters thick.

Finally, after a last pass—small airplanes checking the damage—the noise stopped. But we could hear the crackling and roaring of the flames that spread quickly even as we thought that calm had returned. The incendiary bombs had done their destructive work. There was nothing left of the refinery but an immense heap of bricks and scrap iron. Only the part of the stable adjoining our houses was spared. Seven soldiers were killed, and three workers—friends of Auguste—died as they sought shelter. There were also fifty wounded.

During the following days, people went to the refinery as to a show; the sight of the ruins left them incredulous. The nearby countryside was in chaos. One could actually get lost in the mess. To find the railroad station, one had to look for broken-up railroad cars, half-buried, because the station itself had been blown off the map. Not a tree, not a bush—only the dug-up earth which had swallowed the macadam road and the side streets.

This meant the closing of the refinery and the departure of Captain Schmidt, of no use now for running the ruins. Pépé continued to work for the company, caring for the horses in the part of the stable that still stood. He cleared rubble and began rebuilding. Mr. Hiet, the agent, had been wounded. He was moved to the town of Mitry by the company, but he had to leave there several months after the Liberation.

Our son, Auguste, came to see us regularly. His arm continued to worry us. He had a lot of pain, barely soothed by the pills prescribed by the doctor. He found his work at the brick factory very difficult, but able-bodied men were rare at that time, so he was kept on anyway. The shortage of male laborers was also felt at the farm. I even returned to the fields again, especially during the wheat and sugar-beet harvests.

My boss became more depressed each day, talking little, wild with worry about her husband. She had heard nothing except that, after being imprisoned at Compiègne, he had been condemned as a terrorist and now he was in prison somewhere in Germany.

At the Kuppas' place, a bar called derisively "le Café Français," the Germans led a boisterous life. Late at night, we could hear loud music. The Polish woman was soon consoled for her husband's death. Those who weren't afraid peered through the curtains in the evening. They said it was a nightly orgy, with women from Paris, made up like dolls, dancing nude on the tables. The city was scandalized by this spectacle, when so many people were suffering. Pépé was more philosophical: "There have always been sluts, there always will be. We'll never change that." Nevertheless, that didn't stop him from thinking that it was highly immoral.

For some time, we had been better informed about the real situation. We had a good little radio that we had bought from Camus, the radio electrician. Each evening, taking precautions like conspirators, we plugged up all the holes in our walls and listened to London, which we recognized because it sounded like a coffee mill. So we learned the true news. We never trusted Radio Paris, which reported any old thing. One evening, we heard about the landing in France. The Germans became more and more cantankerous as the English news grew optimistic.

One night, we were wakened with a start by a loud explosion followed by gunfire. Pépé wanted to go out and see what it was, but I didn't let him. In the morning, we learned that the Kommandatur had been badly damaged by a bomb placed in a greenhouse behind it. Two men at the guard post had been killed.

The incident had no consequences for several days. No one saw the Gestapo, busy elsewhere, no doubt. It looked as though the German army was becoming disorganized.

About then, I had a terrible scare. It was a Sunday morning, and we had just returned from mass. I was preparing lunch—my son was coming to eat with us that day—when someone knocked roughly on the door. I went to open it and found myself nose to nose with a helmeted Boche, a rifle on his back. He gave me a paper. Pépé had to go immediately to the Kommandatur. My legs quaked, and I felt ill. The soldier insistently repeated a German word that I didn't know. It was as though he wanted to reassure me. Pépé didn't feel very courageous. I clung to him as if I would never see him again. I thought of my boss. But my husband hadn't done anything, I was sure of it. He had told me so.

He left with the soldier. I sat in the kitchen, incapable of going back to the stove. Auguste, my son, arrived at that moment. He was pale, having passed his father and his escort. He began to watch at the door, and that lasted at least an hour. It was definitely the longest hour of my life.

I imagined Pépé, beaten and tortured, thrown into a cell at the Kommandatur, where people said terrible things happened. Suddenly, Auguste turned to me, smiling and relieved: "Here he is, Mother," I felt better right away. And my Pépé actually arrived, calm, but with a drawn face. "It was about the horses," he explained. "I have to take them to headquarters tomorrow morning at six o'clock."

He fell silent. Poor old Percherons. Faithful companions, where would they be taken? All day long that Sunday, my husband moped around sadly. Pépé didn't yet know that his Percherons would save his life.

He left with the four animals the next day, at 5:30, so he wouldn't be late. He was let in through the carriage entrance of the German headquarters so that he could tether the horses in the park.

He had been gone for about half an hour when I heard the sound of trucks and cars, followed by short orders barked in German. Before I could stand up to see what was happening, the door was shoved open with blows from rifle butts. Men dressed in black uniforms burst into the room. They looked everywhere, without a word, even down in the cellar, and then left brusquely, just as they had come. They did the same in each house of our *coron*. The soldiers—we were told later that it was the S.S.—broke in with rifle-butt blows and forced all the men out, guns in the small of their backs, even the very young ones. Some were barely sixteen. They did the same thing on the main street, seizing men randomly as they left for work. They forced twenty-one who were taken to the road out of the village, in the direction of Paris. And there, on the side of the road, barely aware of what was happening, the village men were slaughtered by volleys of machine-gun fire.

I heard the gunshots, and I was wild with worry for my husband, and for my son as well. The latter, luckily for him, was working the night shift at the brickworks; otherwise he would have been killed too. As for Pépé, he was getting ready to return, distressed at having to leave his horses, when he heard the noise of trucks and the shouts. A young, very blond soldier told him gently, "You, monsieur, you wait here. Forbidden to leave."

At the same moment, several meters away, the S.S. were seizing the village men.

This massacre caused deep mourning for a long time. When the Americans arrived several days later, there was little joy, less enthusiasm from us than elsewhere. Many families were in mourning. They couldn't celebrate because their husband, their son, or their brother was no more. That was the case in our *coron*, where ten men—both young and old—had been executed senselessly, when they had done nothing.

In Mitry, an American motorcycle soldier was killed in front of the Kommandatur by some Germans who were de-

• *Mémé Santerre* •

fending it, but they surrendered soon afterward. They came out with their hands in the air to the hooting and spitting of the townspeople, who were avenging themselves, such as they could, for their anguish and misery. At the same time, men with tricolored armbands emerged from all over—the Resistance, from what people said. I would never have believed that there were so many in our little town.

The first thing that some of them did was to run to the Café Français to drag out, with kicks in the ass, the girls and their proprietor, who hadn't had time to flee. Poor girls! They were forced to march around the town-hall square, amid insults and slaps, and their heads were shaved by makeshift barbers. Pépé, who was there, came home scandalized. "They are whores, that's for sure. But so what? I don't think it's ever honorable for men to treat women like that."

According to him, the women collaborators should have been imprisoned and tried by a judge. Parading them naked through the streets like that was wrong.

The men collaborators were gathered together at the town hall. They were also treated roughly. But it wasn't the same. They were men, and they were getting only what they deserved.

One person whom I was very content to see punished was Kuppa's wife, whom they took to prison in Melun. Ah! I didn't feel sorry for her, even though she too had her head shaved. It was impossible for her not to have known of the dirty tricks her husband played. I thought of my boss, whom she had betrayed, of her triumphant air when she sat enthroned at her café during the Occupation, in the midst of all the German soldiers. A court condemned her to death. Surely they had plenty of proof of her evil deeds. That was the last consolation for my poor boss's wife. She died soon after she received the official telegram telling her that her husband had died in Dachau during the winter of 1943.

138

Some months had passed since the Liberation. We were
seriously worried about our son's health. One day Pépé and I
walked around the site of the refinery, which was almost completely cleared. Ten years of our lives had passed. Ruins and
sorrow surrounded us. The two of us were growing old. Pépé
only rarely called me "Marie-Cat." He preferred "Mémé," as
everyone else called me. Our hair had turned gray without our
noticing. When we thought of our parents, it seemed that it
was only yesterday that they had lived with us and the day
before yesterday when we had lived with them. Pépé and I
walked arm in arm while old memories—memories both
happy and sad—followed in a parade behind us. My husband
stopped, looking at me. Then he said, smiling, "You know,
Mémé, really, a life isn't very long."

Chapter Ten

For many months we lived with the rumble of tractors, which were rebuilding the refinery not far from where we lived. The stable and a vast garage were erected first, while the rail line was being restored nearby. Temporary huts were put up in place of the sugar-beet storehouses. So, here and there, life began again.

The company again bought the farm, which they had sold several years earlier, hoping, I guess, that business would be better after the long poverty of the war. Distant relatives of my dead boss closed the deal without any haggling, because they needed the money in a hurry.

A new, very young agent arrived, who had graduated from a big agricultural college. He was extraordinary, that boy—he even predicted the harvests by complicated calculations in his office. Tractors and modern equipment were received. But, to Pépé's great joy, the company also sent three horses—three handsome Ardennais—which arrived in vans one morning.

I continued to work in the kitchen, and Pépé joined me at the farm to take charge of the stable, since the work at the refinery was all reconstruction. The agent wanted him to learn to drive tractors, but my husband could never do it. He was afraid of engines. He preferred his horses, of which he could be certain, and the new boss didn't insist.

Times sure had changed. The agent had two assistants: there were three men where before there had been only one! Also, the year-round workers lived in the village, not at the farm. The age of live-in farm workers was past. The agent abolished Sunday shifts and, even at the height of the harvest, no one had to work that day. The wheat and the sugar beets could wait.

We had our first real vacations then. Three weeks with nothing to do, for Pépé and me to look each other in the whites of our eyes. We couldn't get over it! We got a coupon from the town hall that gave us a discount on a one-week stay in the mountains, but we refused. We were scared to go and live in a hotel. We weren't used to it. Also, Auguste's health troubled us. He had stopped working at the brick factory because they no longer needed him, once able-bodied workers returned. He received only a small social-security pension for his paralysis; his left arm didn't move at all anymore and was very painful. He was given endless shots to ease the pain.

In 1955, our pension file was set up and we were given forms to fill out for the pensions we had earned. In 1956, we retired. We didn't get much, but we had enough to live on.

Ah! Those first days of retirement, they were something! We couldn't believe it. Pépé was up at dawn, moving around the kitchen. As for me, when I woke up, I jumped instinctively out of bed as I had for half a century. Then I would remember and snuggle back down in the well-warmed sheets. I had time. Pépé would come tiptoeing into the bedroom, asking me if I was sick, sleeping so late!

Restlessly, he would dress himself and go walk in the huge fields he knew so well, examining the soil, talking with the workers he met on the plain. They all respected my Pépé very much. He was such a fine man.

This life of laziness bothered him. Of course, he had our garden behind the house, but the work on that was soon done. Anyway, we soon lost that, among other things. We had continued to live in company housing, but a letter came from Paris advising us that we had one month to vacate to make room for workers at the refinery, finally completed. They reminded us that we were retired and no longer had the right to company lodgings.

I went to the town hall in Mitry to find out what could be done. Houses for rent were rare, but I knew that a housing development was being built, a whole new city near the common. A social worker took care of our case. I was never comfortable filling out papers, and poor Pépé was no help, not knowing how to read or write.

Several weeks later, we were assigned an apartment. Just in time. We had been receiving letters from the company, threatening to evict us. The mayor of Mitry, a Communist, got angry, and one day he sent a letter on the town letterhead to the company. He told them firmly that after employing people for a half-century, they shouldn't be so stingy about an extra month of lodging.

I went with Pépé to see the apartment we were getting in the new development. The tall brick and stone buildings were still being built. Workers were laying out the lawns, and, inside, we could hear the last hammer blows of the men finishing the installation.

We were among the first to move in, on the ground floor on the left. When I entered the apartment through the little hall, I thought I was in the kitchen and looked for the bedroom. But there wasn't one. It was what they called a studio. The kitchen was about as big as a closet. On the other hand, we had a little bathroom and central heating.

I quickly realized that we couldn't fit all our furniture in there. It wasn't that we had much, but the studio was so small! We had to sell some of it. The moving was quickly done. A tractor and trailer sent by the young agent at the farm, on his own responsibility, transported our bed, a cupboard, and a table. There we were, within our new walls, feeling lost.

It was then that we learned about kindness—from our neighbors. They were all simple people whose circumstances were very modest. But, for the first time in our lives, we weren't alone anymore. Mothers, who probably had enough to do with their broods, came to see us. The first day, one of them brought us dinner, a lamb stew in a pot. That evening, her husband and eldest son came to help move our furniture.

It was comforting to have these men, so strong and cheerful, around us. We were less upset when we went to bed. The lamb had been so good that we had tears in our eyes when we ate it.

Each day we learned more about our neighbors, who had their little money troubles. They spoke constantly about budgets and inflation. Yet when we needed them, they forgot their worries and came to help us.

We were soon Pépé and Mémé to everyone. We didn't know how to thank them for their friendship. Pépé, who was bored, began to do favors for one or the other. We rented a worker's garden in a nearby field, and my husband ran it and those of our neighbors, to keep busy. A friend taught me to knit, and I knitted little socks for layettes with the wool people brought me. The mothers' gratitude was my pay. We felt useful despite our age. Children came to see us, and their piping voices were a source of extra happiness for us.

So, bit by bit, we got used to this universe of public housing. The buildings that blocked our view on all sides bothered us less, even though all our lives we had had the infinity of the plains before our eyes. It was nice and warm in our little studio, and we didn't have to worry about keeping a fire going. And then there was the bathroom, with hot water all the time. All our lives, we had washed ourselves each day in a basin of water, going by "sections," wetting our bodies as we progressed. One had to be fanatic about cleanliness, as Pépé and I were, not to let oneself go in such conditions. But we were stubborn about it, and everywhere we lived, our first concern was to have a private corner in which we could wash ourselves completely.

So baths were a true blessing from the very beginning! The first day, Pépé was so comfortable that he fell asleep in the tub. I discovered him there, nude, snoring like a horn player in the soapy water.

Our life was easy from then on. We even succeeded in putting money aside. Pépé, always busy in his garden, grew quantities of vegetables. We had so many that we gave them away—leeks, cabbages, carrots, and herbs. He even grew endives in boxes of sand in the basement. It was a great event in the building when he harvested those vegetables. But the superintendent forbade him to go any further, perhaps fearing he would build mushroom beds there too.

We would have been happy if it hadn't been for our concern for our son, who declined each day in terrible pain. He received medical care, but it couldn't give him relief. It was torture for us that our only son should die like this, with no way for us to help him. When God finally delivered him, he was only fifty-three. I was seventy-three, and I told myself that the world was upside down when children died before their parents. He died one evening, soothed at the end by the large doses of morphine they gave him. How brokenhearted we were as we took him to the cemetery, where we had bought a plot for the three of us.

My daughter-in-law, whom I never liked, also felt much sorrow, but Pépé and I were immersed in ours. On our return, we wept for a long time, evoking very old memories. How Auguste, in Avay, began going to school, where I escorted him with the strap and he had run away saying, "Maman, hide your strap! I don't want my friends to see it." How pleased he had been at his apprenticeship with Berger, the barber, and how proud when he brought home a few sous. Poor Auguste, who had been taken away from us so young! It seemed to us at the time that we had lost part of our bodies—an arm, a leg, something that was part of us—which we would miss forever.

After that, we had a place to walk: the cemetery. There we would stroll slowly, looking at the gravestones of the unknown people lying there. All of them had loved, hoped, and struggled before finally rotting beneath a stone.

Several months later, we had a surprise. Our immediate neighbor, the one who had the five-room apartment next door, came and rang our doorbell. He had a television set in his arms. "Here, Mémé, it's for you. We are going to buy a new one. And for the price they would give me for that one, I would rather have you enjoy it than make some shopkeeper rich."

I was dumbfounded, as was Pépé when he came home. So it came about that we had a TV too, and the set worked well. It helped us endure the pain that had struck us. One Sunday I made a beautiful cake and Pépé bought a bottle of champagne, a real indulgence. We invited the neighbors. What a fête! Even Pépé, who didn't drink alcohol, wanted to taste the champagne. We had never drunk it and didn't know how it tasted. It resembled lemonade and, to top that, it wasn't even sugared, so we were disappointed. But we were content—that was the important thing—because our neighbors were so kind!

Our life went on like that, marked by our strolls to the cemetery and evenings watching television. I knitted for hours while Pépé was gardening or going from friend to friend doing small chores. My little wool socks were a hit. My reputation spread throughout the development, and mothers came to visit me. I didn't want to be paid. It wasn't necessary; we had enough to live on.

Instead, I was always getting little presents—trinkets, souvenirs from vacations—and my buffet was soon covered with these knickknacks. They were my pride and joy. There were little music boxes, shells, miniature porcelain statues, boxes of candy, a barometer, plates. I had a collection of "Souvenir of . . ." that my "clients" brought me from the sea or the mountains. Also, colored postcards addressed to Pépé and Mémé Santerre, which they sent us in the summer months. We knew where everyone was that way, and we amused ourselves by looking at those far-off countrysides and cities which we had never seen ourselves.

Pépé went to his garden almost every day. He had bought a wheelbarrow and, early in the morning, he set out to spade, hoe, or sow. When he had finished his plot, he would go to those of our neighbors. He always had something to do and never stopped for a minute. After a while, he—who had never been tired—began to seem fatigued to me.

One evening, to my great astonishment, he refused to take coffee. I was incredulous. Coffee filled an important place in our lives. We drank it ten times a day—for a yes, for a no— nice and hot, and sugary. It was our luxury. The enameled percolator was always waiting on the gas burner. And there was Pépé refusing a cup! "I don't know what's wrong, but my stomach burns endlessly these days," he told me. And he added, smiling, "It's nothing. It will pass."

The first time, I gave him mint tea, but in the following weeks the burning continued. He felt strange ticklings, practically continuously, which were followed by disagreeable sensations of intense heat. Was it the illness that was tiring him out? He went to the garden less. He couldn't carry his watering can without burning sensations that were soon followed by pains.

We tried an arsenal of bottles and tubes of medicine, and all had no effect. He still complained of pain, so I began to worry seriously. We called a doctor. It was Dr. S. The neighbors recommended him. He came as soon as we called him, at any hour of day or night.

He examined Pépé at length, silently. He assured me that the heart, the lungs, the reflexes were excellent. He prescribed a diet without salt or fat and capsules to be taken five times a day.

When Pépé told him about his garden, the doctor was explicit. Pépé was forbidden to work in it. "You are sound, Mr. Santerre, but you are tired. You must rest."

For a while, the burning stopped. Not completely, of course; my husband still felt the unpleasant tickling. On the other hand, he didn't have much pain anymore. Cautiously, he took out his wheelbarrow to go to his corner of earth, where he so enjoyed himself. But he didn't stay long. "Really," he said when he came back, "I am nothing but an old carcass, an old beast. I can't even raise the watering can anymore."

The pain began again, more and more intense. Pépé held his stomach with both hands when the red-hot iron that consumed his insides began an attack. We went back to Dr. S. By the end of 1971, the doctor was coming three or four times a week. He tried all sorts of treatments; then he ordered a long series of examinations, blood tests, x-rays, et cetera.

Medications succeeded medications. Quantities, in tubes, in bottles, in envelopes, in boxes. They invaded the buffet, where I arranged them, after they had proved to be ineffective. None soothed my poor Pépé, whose pain gave him less and less respite.

The struggle continued, step by step. First, my husband gave up going out. Then even the simple comings and goings in the room became unbearable. He settled down in the Voltaire chair, an old armchair that came from his parents, whose common room it had dominated for years. Toward the month of October, he could no longer leave the chair except to go painfully to our bed. Then that became impossible.

The parade of medications continued. When Pépé was incapable of getting up, Dr. S. prescribed shots, which were given by a nurse, first one, then two, then three, then four times a day.

Until then, my husband had slept pretty well. Alas, sleep became impossible and life became hell. Nights were pierced with cries of suffering that I was unable to calm. I couldn't stand it any longer. I was coming and going like a sleepwalker, my hair unkempt, my eyes reddened, dazed by fatigue.

The neighbors kept coming over. They helped me as much as they could by running my errands. I no longer had the time to go shopping. All the wives were shocked when they saw my husband in his bed. In two months, the disease had transformed his face, distorting it with stabs of needle-sharp pain, and the wrinkles grew a bit deeper every day.

In December, a few days before my eightieth birthday, Dr. S. gave up trying to cure Auguste. The tests had all been negative, with no clear results. All the prescribed treatments had been ineffective.

He suggested hospitalization . . . for both of us! I was only the shadow of myself, and since I was never fat, that really wasn't much. I shriveled, grew thinner, drunk with weariness. I became obsessed with the thought of sleep, once my Pépé had found shelter, cared for by nurses. Sometimes, furious at my inability to calm him, I hugged him tightly. It seemed that it should be soothing to be held against me. But it was even worse. His cries redoubled and I had to lay him back on the pillow, sobbing. In the evening, when he finally fell asleep for a bit, I went down on my knees and prayed. On Pépé's chest, I touched the little cloth bag holding a medal of the Virgin. It was the one that Uncle Sulphart had given me so long ago; I in turn had given it to my husband on our wedding day. It seemed as if I could make our good God hear me better if I held the medallion.

What a sad day my birthday was! All over the town, people were getting ready for Christmas. In living-room picture windows, one could see the glowing multicolored lights on

Christmas trees, and people came and went through the halls of the apartment building carrying packages. There was a joyous bustle everywhere, but our little studio was gloomy and sad. Dr. S. came around 8:00 and gave my husband a shot. He said gently, "It's my Christmas present, Mrs. Santerre, the only one that I can give him."

Pépé slept profoundly, calmly. Around us, I heard songs, music, the sound of television. I thought of previous Christmases. Very simple Christmases: leaving for mass in the night in Avesnes, our return celebrated with good hot chicory. At our neighbor's, the railroad worker's, it was practically silent. Although our walls touched, I heard only hushed voices. I appreciated them more than ever that evening, those good people who kept their children quiet, even though they were impatient to see their toys.

Then I heard a well-loved song. One often heard it on the radio Christmas Eve, and Pépé hummed it sometimes. No doubt the neighbors had gently increased the volume on the radio to send us that tune as a sign of friendship.

> *Silent night, holy night,*
> *All is calm, all is bright,*
> *Round yon virgin mother and child,*
> *Holy infant so tender and mild,*
> *Sleep in heavenly peace,*
> *Sleep in heavenly peace.*

May God forgive me! That song was the drop of water that overflowed the bucket. All my troubles rose together in a flood: the sorrows of the past, those of the present. My heart—which was so full of sadness, a mixture of memories of my parents, of my poor son—my heart released the sorrow that had swelled in it for months. And I began to cry as I have never again cried, slowly, without choking or sobbing, an inexhaustible river of tears that finally soothed me.

As I fell into a deep sleep near Pépé, who snored, knocked
out by the shot, I heard the joyous pealing of the church bells
which called the faithful to come celebrate the advent of the
Son of God. Yes, it was Christmas! In all that, what did two
poor old people matter, lying next to each other in the dark?

Chapter Eleven

The siren of the ambulance caused a stir in our neighborhood. It was parked at our door, flying a Red Cross flag. Going to the window, I read on the white side: MEAUX HOSPITAL. ORGEMONT ANNEX.

That was my future domicile. I certainly did not foresee that I would never return to our little studio with my Pépé. Two big fellows carried him out of our house on a stretcher, gently but hurriedly. It was December 26. They came, they left, there was no time to look back. Across the frosty plains of Brie, I took the longest ride I had made since my arrival in Mitry, excepting the exodus of 1940. The two-tone ambulance siren sounded constantly, warning those ahead as we sped down the icy road. A rotating blue light flashed on the roof.

Finally we reached Meaux, where I glimpsed the tall square tower of the cathedral through windows clouded by the heat inside the ambulance. As we went toward the city, the car made a sudden turn to the left, skidding as it turned. There came a ramp, and then I saw the big buildings, their roofs white with ice, surrounded by immense hedges and trees, bare at that season. They gave a sense of calm and security. I instinctively knew that we would be well cared for here. The ambulance continued its slippery voyage on the icy road and stopped before a long building of yellow brick and stone with immense glass doors. A plaque said: GENERAL MEDICINE. DR. HAPPERT'S SERVICE.

So it was that I first saw the name of the man who rapidly became my friend and for whom I have ever since felt boundless admiration. I met him almost immediately. He was very strong, very reassuring in his white coat. His face impressed me, a face of infinite goodwill, with eyes usually smiling behind his glasses.

"Come, Mémé," he said, squeezing my shoulder gently, "don't get upset; we will take good care of your husband." And he added, "But you too need to recuperate. You can't stand up anymore." I was taken by a nurse across a big hall with a terrazzo floor, scattered with large armchairs and decorated with green plants, to the right side, the women's section. The ambulance attendants disappeared to the left, with Pépé on a stretcher. We went down a very long, well-lighted corridor. The walls were brightly painted, and each room had a metal number on the door. Here and there, women in white walked around, pushing little carts carrying bottles and metal basins.

It was medication time. I was put in a very large room with two beds, whose tall windows looked out on the garden. The other patient slept soundly. My arrival didn't trouble her at all. We didn't meet each other until two hours later, when she woke up.

I was put to bed, and I began to wait. For what? I didn't know, but that's how it was. One was always on the lookout in that universe, sonorous and silent in turn, with its strange odors, some more, some less agreeable. There were the perfume of soap, the strong smell of ether, whiffs of food at mealtimes. The passage of the nurses' aides with their arsenals

of sponges and basins, that of the nurses with trays of medications were events to anticipate.

I rapidly learned not to show any curiosity about my case.
On the other hand, I was worried about Pépé. For the first
time in ages, we were separated. That hadn't happened since
the beginning of our marriage, when he went to the country.
Then the doctor and his assistants arrived, giving me hope: I
would finally find out.

As usual, however, I got no news to show for the visit. Still,
the comforting presence of Dr. Happert leaning over me was a
great help. He listened to my insides at length, while around
him everyone was finally quiet. "You're fine," he told me
cheerfully. "You must rest and regain your strength so you can
go visit your husband over there."

Then it seemed that his voice became more serious and his
air more worried. I questioned him anxiously. "What does he
have, Doctor? Tell me, I beg you."

"Don't worry. He is being tested. We'll see what he has and
we will treat it. But it will be slow, very slow. You must have
patience." With those words, he pulled my blanket back up
and tapped my cheeks. Then the good doctor disappeared in
his train of questions and answers.

After lunch, I fell into lethargy. My nerves relaxed. No
doubt I had been given a drug. After my last mouthful, I fell
onto the pillow, knocked out.

I was awakened from my sleep early by the carts rolling in
the corridors. All along their route, one could hear the sound
of coughs and voices. Complaints, too, all the difficult and
painful awakenings of the suffering bodies that lay there. The
night had given them several hours of respite, brought on by
shots and sedatives, but now it was past.

Next to me, my neighbor had opened her eyes. She didn't
talk, seeming not to see me. I was frightened by the strange
fixity of her look, empty and distant. I rose to wash myself.
Outside a gray day began to dawn, so I could see the icy bushes

153

that looked like big white balls. The nurses' aides were busy
with my neighbor, putting clean sheets on her bed which had
the bitter, hot odor of freshly ironed linen. They worked
quickly, moving her body without one excess motion. She was
maneuvered like a doll, without the least roughness, but with
a confidence that suggested much experience. My bed was
straightened. I was washed and rubbed with eau de cologne. I
felt much better, rested, although I continued to be always
anxious about Pépé.

I lay back down and resumed my waiting. Around 8:00, the
little carts arrived, in a clatter of jugs of milk and coffee. Ah,
it seemed good, that bowl of coffee, good and hot, well-
sugared, with rusks buttered to the edge, which the nurse
served with a nice smile. "Here, Grandmother, this will do
you good."

You can bet that that did me good! Emboldened by the
niceness of that young woman, I inquired about Pépé. But she
didn't know. The men were far away, on the other side of the
building, and the staff wasn't the same. Still, a nurse who
came later gave me some news. My husband had slept well,
without any distress.

That reassured me a little. I decided to get up to go to the
window. They had said that I could. Outside, it was terribly
cold. One could see muffled-up people passing by, hurrying
toward the heated buildings. I stood there for a moment,
when all of a sudden, without warning, I felt dizzy and crum-
pled up, unconscious.

I was told later that I had had a mild heart attack and must
rest in bed for several days. When I regained consciousness,
my room had been changed. The neighboring bed was empty.

The nurses and the nurses' aides were very kind. They
quickly baptized me "little Mémé." Dr. Happert called me
that too. But some days, when he saw that I was sad, he
cheered me up by saying "my dear" or "my beautiful princess."

As soon as I felt better and could walk a little in the corridors, I asked for permission to go see Pépé.

Every afternoon I went to his room, a room like mine. I thought he looked better. His face was more relaxed but, on the other hand, it was yellow. I was so happy to know he was better! We stayed there together for hours, the two of us, hand in hand, without talking much, to avoid tiring him. The nurses watched him carefully, and there were always medications to swallow and the sacred temperature to be taken. At the hospital, the thermometer is the commander-in-chief. Morning and evening, the thermometer reading on the graph paper posted at the foot of your bed indicated your state of health for the day.

One day I was overjoyed to see him sitting in an armchair. His health continued to improve, except for the tint of his skin. We began to be reassured, talking again of our return to Mitry, when he was cured, as if it were a certainty.

Little by little, I became acquainted with the staff of the hospital and my neighbors from nearby rooms. From time to time, we would have a little chat in one of our rooms, but not a long one. The supervising nurse wouldn't stand for that. It disturbed the routine.

There was also a common room where we could get together to sew, to read and talk. Some watched television in the evening. I didn't like to go much. It was endless gossip— the women never stopped talking of their illnesses, which made me uneasy. They never stopped, because the impulse to describe and complain was stronger than they were. They were forever discussing their treatments or their operations.

In all this conversation, the husband's name turned up regularly. There were more or less flattering comments, depending on the atmosphere of the household. "He's a good worker, but he doesn't do anything around the house." . . . "He doesn't care about anything, as long as the meal is ready when he gets home." . . . "Oh, him, I can't complain. He keeps busy with lots of things. Luckily!" . . . "He never stops asking the doctor when I will return. The house needs cleaning!" Each woman thus revealed her worries in her conversation.

There were some who were really sneaky. They felt fine, but when their husbands came to visit, they began to whine. Some even took their acting further and got back into bed.

Those poor husbands! They arrived with a bouquet of flowers, or oranges or cookies or candies. They were awkward, loaded down by their packages. They brought news about the family, about the house. "Yes, of course, I am managing! But I still would like you to return soon." . . . "No, no, don't worry. It's all right. But Nénette broke a cup from our good china, one with the gold flowers." . . . "It was hilarious! I tried to make crêpes yesterday evening. I'll be damned, but I couldn't find the flour." . . . "You must try to hurry home. Not on my account, but because of the kids. They're all upset." . . . "But no, but no . . . Don't worry so; we are managing as well as we can."

The husbands left, having brought their news, concerned not to have forgotten anything. For them, what was most important was knowing their wife's discharge date. The world of the hospital is strange. He or she who is inside its walls quickly loses the notion of what's important outside. Everything was related to oneself, to one's health, to one's treatment, occasionally to the medical history of the neighbor.

As I never had stories to tell, everyone rapidly began to use me as a confidante. There was a regular parade through my room. Even the nurses began to tell me their troubles and their little affairs of the heart. "Go see Mémé Santerre," they said. "She is always cheerful. She will boost your spirits."

In this routinized little world, the big events were often arrivals or departures. A bag was packed the day before, and the husband arrived to fetch the long-awaited wife. He swept her away with a wealth of concern, having come to measure her value in the home quite precisely in the days, or some-times weeks, she had been gone.

Others brought their wives in. They were worried, lost at having to leave her there, all alone, unable to tear themselves away after settling her in, often consoling her with, "Don't worry, I'll come back tomorrow." As if to imply that their visit would straighten everything out, which, alas, was not always the case.

Several days after our arrival, our neighbors visited me. They brought clean clothes, cookies, candies. Everything was fine in our studio, which the young woman had cleaned from bottom to top. That reassured me. Among the things they brought, I was pleased to see Pépé's wool nightcap. I had completely forgotten it when we left, and that had distressed me. He never slept without that cap, which kept his head warm. I brought it to him that very day, and he had it from then on.

I was feeling better also, so I bought wool through a nurse, white wool with which I knitted little socks. I made presents for those who had babies, and they were just as successful as in Mitry. People came to compliment me and admire my knit-ting. Soon I couldn't meet the demand. I knitted and knitted, happy to make myself useful amid the boring life of the hospi-tal and the gossip about this or that person.

So our daily course went on, and, although it wasn't really normal, Pépé and I got used to it. It didn't last long. After a respite of a couple of weeks, my husband began to have pain again. He was able to sit in his armchair only three times. What continued to surprise me was his complexion, which grew more and more yellow.

I was told only a couple of things about his disease. Dr. Happert was evasive, and I finally decided that Pépé had jaundice, because of the color of his skin. It was hard to believe. He slept most of the time, even when I visited. When he awoke, he didn't seem to be aware of his surroundings; he was in pain constantly. Through it all, his eyes—his luminous blue eyes—remained strong, despite his debilitating struggle for life. Then his condition improved again. For some time, he was given intravenous injections several times a day. Radical treatment was being tried, a nurse told me. In about a month, Pépé regained his appetite. Above all, his skin became less yellow. I was near him morning, noon, and night, thanks to the kindness of the staff, because it was out of the ordinary, as I well knew.

The months passed, very long and very short at the same time. I felt better, completely rested and recuperated. Still, when I spoke of leaving, the doctor said I had to rest more so that I would completely recover. At the time, I didn't understand why he wanted me there: because he expected what I didn't know enough to fear, being completely reassured about my husband's health.

About that time, I got a new roommate. Her name was Margot, a very sweet young woman who was being treated for her nerves. She and I became friends right away. She didn't like the gossip of the other women either, and we often stayed in our room to be undisturbed. I knitted; she read. Sometimes I described my life, and she began to take an interest in Pépé. I gave her the news every day. It did me good, the presence of this attentive young woman who talked little, listened a lot, and always found the right words to console me when my husband wasn't doing well.

On September 19, Auguste turned eighty-four. I brought him some flowers and a little tart, but he couldn't eat it. From then on, it was the final decline, the ultimate combat of that poor man who couldn't suffer anymore. Finally, I learned the truth. One day the terrible word rang in my ears like a death knell, destroying my remaining illusions: Pépé had cancer of the pancreas!

The doctor explained that everything had been tried except an operation. The surgeon had refused to operate because of my husband's age and his poor condition in general. Sixty-two laboratory tests and ten radiation treatments had been prescribed in the attempt to confine the disease, to close in on it, and maybe to conquer it, but in vain. There was nothing left except painkillers. Then, gambling all or nothing, the doctor had prescribed high doses of cortisone in intravenous shots. That was when Pépé seemed better and began to eat practically normally, hardly suffering any pain. He owed a respite of a couple of months to this treatment. Then the awful disease regained the upper hand, continuing its ravages inside his body, slowly, inexorably. He was given shots regularly to keep him from suffering too much pain. I stayed to watch him, my poor man.

While I held his hand, his voice echoed in my memory. "So, Marie-Catherine, how are you today? . . . I am very pleased, you know, Marie-Cat, that you have given me a son. . . . You're not too tired, are you?"

On October 29, 1973, in the evening, I had just left him when someone came to get me. "Come quickly! Grandpa's not well at all."

I knew that he was dead. I hurried to his room, assisted by the nurse. Dr. Happert was there. He rubbed my cheek in a gesture of great fondness. Then he disappeared, along with his staff. I was alone with my husband. The little cloth bag containing the medallion of the Virgin was outside his nightshirt. It had been placed in his crossed hands. An extraordinary peace had descended upon his face; the disappearance of his intolerable pain had rejuvenated his features. He looked transfigured.

I began to pray and weep. I stayed there for hours, by my Pépé. Much later, a nurse came to put me to bed with a sedative. Margot was there. She was the last person I saw, bent over me as I sank into sleep. I was a widow.

Chapter Twelve

Go to the window, Mémé, you will see him pass by."
Margot took me to the big bay window. She hugged me
against her. In the garden, the dead leaves were gathering
before being caught by the wind and whirled here and there.
We waited in silence.

Finally the long black car emerged from the drive. Pépé was
making his last trip, and what pained me even more was that
he was making it alone. I had instructed them to put on his
handsome Sunday suit, and I had seen him placed in the
coffin. But that had caused me such a shock that I had been
forbidden to go in the car to Mitry. So he left, my poor friend,
to rejoin his son in our tomb. I followed the hearse until it was
swallowed up as it went down the hill.

Luckily, Margot was with me. I felt her there, gentle and
attentive. She laid me down and consoled me as well as she
could. Her presence helped, while I followed Pépé in my
imagination to the cemetery, where he was to be buried close
to Auguste. If only it would be my turn soon! What would
become of me without him, after sixty-four years of living

together, one with the other, without any disagreement, not a single argument?

Dr. Happert watched me closely. He came alone many times, in addition to his visits with the students. As a doctor who rubbed elbows with death every day, he tried hard to cheer me up. "You must think of yourself now, my dear. We are going to cure you—quickly, in a flash!" And he would depart, leaving behind him a big breath of optimism. When did I begin to smile once again at his pleasantries? I don't remember; I was a bit ashamed at first. But it was stronger than me: one couldn't continue to be forlorn with that man, so brave, so happy.

As long as he was there, and Margot too (although she left several weeks after my husband died), I could bear my loss pretty well. I felt recovered, strong enough to return to Mitry and my little apartment.

Dr. Happert was fooled too, or at least I think he was. He let me go after one last test. My blood pressure was normal, and I felt much better.

I left after Christmas, a very sad Christmas that had no meaning. The Christmas of a widow in the hospital—what could be more awful?

The ambulance drove me back home, and its siren alerted the neighborhood. I was immediately surrounded by friends. I was settled into the apartment, where everything was spotless, scrubbed by my nice neighbor. Then I was alone in my little studio. For the first time, I realized the extent of my loss. Everything in the room reminded me of Pépé and our life, each minute of it so completely shared. For many years, we hadn't left each other for an instant. He was next to me and I was next to him.

The day after my return to Mitry, I asked to be taken to the cemetery. What an expedition! I could barely walk and had to be supported to the grave. I had expected some comfort from this visit, but things became even worse. Knowing he was so close there under the earth was another heartbreak. Since he couldn't rejoin me, wouldn't it be best for me to go to him? What was there to live for? I was ready to die right away, while I was near the grave, and be buried immediately, without ceremony, without fuss. I had a hard time leaving the gray stone with its big cross under which my two men rested.

I spent an abominable night back at the studio. I couldn't sleep. Visions paraded ceaselessly before my eyes, some very old, others recent. I was an adolescent, refusing to make a couple with Auguste: I didn't want him as godfather because he didn't please me. Then I saw him on the embankment in Avesnes, holding my hand. Suddenly he disappeared to go to the country, and, without a transition, I felt him by my side in bed, not daring to stir because of my parents sleeping below. Then there were the three of us, and Auguste, our son, shaved him and cut his hair.

Then we were sleeping in our house in Avay, and we heard the tocsin and I saw my husband perched on the ladder at the burning farm. And then the departure for Brittany, which I mixed with the exodus of 1940 and the bombing of the sugar refinery: Pépé was running with his horses to get them to shelter.

It seemed as though I was watching a film of my life, but a strange film. It was out of focus, and the scenes were jumbled, one succeeding the other with no continuity. It kept waking me as I began to fall asleep. I slept restlessly, constantly roused by that infernal movie that tore me from my drowsiness.

It lasted for days and days. I had no notion of time. I didn't even want to eat—I wasn't hungry—in that constant malaise. My neighbor came, but at other times I imagined she was there, so I barely noticed her presence. I found food on my table which I hardly touched, herbal teas which I didn't drink. I felt nothing, except the need to think always of my Pépé.

I don't really know how I managed in the studio, when I washed, if I lay down, if I sat, if I went outdoors or not. Outside noises reached me as though from a distance, as if my ears were filled with cotton wool. On the other hand, I very distinctly heard my husband and my son talking to me to reassure me. Real people who came to see me were surrounded by a grayish aura, while Pépé sat there in his armchair. It was he who was present, not the others. I heard murmurs, I saw movement around me, as in a strange and unhealthy dream.

There came a time when I no longer cried. I was transported completely into mysterious surroundings. I didn't feel anything, I wasn't hungry, I wasn't either hot or cold, I didn't really know where I was. Wasn't that my father coming and going? And I was sure that the woman seated over there in the corner was my mother, preparing warps. My brother-in-law Paul arrived in turn with Alfred, his son. He brought me sugar-coated almonds from the baptism. Then Auguste, my husband, bent before me in his wedding suit and took me to visit the Avay refinery, where the barber, Berger, had established his salon. He used the steam from the engines to heat the towels for his clients.

The last scene that I remember was of a struggle, an enormous combat between my husband and a strange animal without head or legs, which nevertheless was biting him in the stomach and then swallowing him slowly, in little bits, while Pépé screamed and screamed. His cries became so excruciating that I thought my skull would burst, and I passed out.

When I came to, I saw the kind face of Dr. Happert, his eyes smiling behind his glasses. He held my wrist; beside him were his interns and nurses. "So, my little Mémé, you collapsed? That's not very nice!"

I don't know how I got back to the hospital in Meaux, but there I was, between the white sheets of a hospital bed. Bit by bit, I regained contact with the outside world. I gradually accustomed myself to thinking of Pépé without feeling cruel pain. My memory of him blurred. I felt relaxed, soothed, comfortable with myself.

It took days and days before I was allowed to get up again or walk through the corridors. I didn't much like going to the men's side. My heart ached when I did. I found newcomers on all sides, women I didn't know. But the gossip was the same, passing from room to room, and the quarrels continued in the television room.

One day, Dr. Happert told me that I was cured but it was out of the question for me to go back home to Mitry. I was to be sent next door to the hospital, to the rest home, whose buildings we could see across from us.

That is where I live today. There are four of us in the room, and we get along well. The room is large and beautiful. It is always nice and warm, and the food is good. The staff is very kind.

My neighbor, Mathilde, is eighty-seven years old, but she calls me "my little Mémé" anyway, like everyone here. Across the room, there are Emilie and Louise. We talk of our little problems, while waiting for visitors.

Some have their children or grandchildren; others have friends or cousins, who bring them a bit of outside news. But this news is no longer ours. We aren't concerned with what happens elsewhere. Still, we pretend to be interested, to avoid hurting anyone's feelings. This way, we learn that there are new deputies and a new president of the Republic. But those important people are far away, very far away.

The important things for us are, in the morning, our hot coffee with rusks and butter and, in the evening, our dinner. There is always muttering when we study our trays. "Stew again!" grumbles Mathilde. "Broth, always broth!" says another, vigorously stirring her bowl. Or, "The cake has fallen flat."

I don't say anything. I think of my past without meat,

without fruit, without cake, and I am very happy. Sometimes it occurs to me that I would be even happier if Pépé were there, and Auguste, my son, too, but the idea is faint, melancholy. My tears are gone, like my laughter, because I know they are useless. One can't struggle against the inevitable. Our life must be accepted as it is, for it is imposed on us. That is what I've tried to make the journalist understand, the one who comes to question me from time to time, asking me to describe my life.

It is December, and this month I will be eighty-four years old. From my window, I watch the garden, where the wind whirls. It is cold, and a white powder falls, sticking to the windows. The bushes are tied together and swept by the wind. I press myself comfortably into my armchair. Silence is all around me. My friends have gone out. My knitting lies on my knees. I am warm, I am well; from the window I wave a friendly adieu to my confessor, the journalist, who has just left me with his tape recorder under his arm. I told him: "All my life, I have done what I had to, the best that I could. I suffered a lot, worked an enormous amount. But above all I have also loved. And, thus, I was happy. So happy that you can never imagine. And happiness, in the end, is all that counts. Now I can die in peace and rejoin my dear ones who wait for me."

Old People's Home
Orgemont Annex
December 1975

Chronology

1891   December 23: Born Marie-Catherine Gardez, in Avesnes-les-Aubert.
1897–1901   Parochial school, Avesnes-les-Aubert.
1901–10, 1914   Seasonal migrations to Normandy, probably Etrépagny.
1909   December 13: Marriage to Auguste Santer (this variant spelling appears on the marriage register).
1911   April 6: Son, Auguste, born in Avesnes-les-Aubert.
1914–18   World War I spent in Normandy working as a servant and laborer on a farm.
1919   Return visit to Avesnes-les-Aubert.
1919–30   Etrépagny, working as a servant on a farm.
1930–56   Mitry (Paris region), working as a servant and occasionally a field laborer on a farm.
1956   Retirement to public housing in Mitry.
1973   Illness, hospitalization, and death of her husband in Meaux; her own hospitalization in Meaux.
1975   Tells her life story to Serge Grafteaux, a Parisian journalist.
1977   February 14: Death in Meaux.

Notes

Introduction

1. See Mona Ozouf, *L'école, l'église, et la République, 1871–1915* (Paris, 1963).

2. John McManners, *Church and State in France* (London, 1971) p. 16.

Chapter One

1. There were twenty sous to a franc.

2. The *coron* is a row of attached brick houses, typical of worker housing in northern France, especially in mining towns. The weavers' *corons* of Avesnes-les-Aubert were on the outskirts of the town, which in 1906 had a population of almost 4,900. Hence, Avesnes was not a village in the strict sense (the French census assigns urban status to agglomerations over 2,000). However, the outskirts of the town in which the *coron* was located were almost rural. Each weaver's cottage had a window to the cellar with a brick arch over it to light the weaving room there.

3. *Tartines* are chunks of bread, cut crosswise.

4. The number of years Mémé went to school is inconsistently given in the text; in this passage, she claimed six.

5. It is not clear if this protest about the expulsion of school-teachers who were members of religious orders had taken place in the first drive (1880s) to laicize the schools (and thus before Mémé's birth) or in 1902–6, when the second laicization drive took place. I was unable to find any account of protest in Avesnes-les-Aubert on clerical issues. The town is located in the Cambrésis, however, a region renowned for its faithful Catholicism. Many more protests occurred against the forced inventories of church property in 1906 than about the schools. See Ozouf and McManners, cited above, and Maurice Larkin, *Church and State after the Dreyfus Affair: The Separation Issue in France* (New York, 1974).

6. The *taille* was the stick on which the record of credit given for bread was recorded by notches.

7. The Gardez family went for a six-month seasonal migration to Normandy. Much of Normandy is presently encompassed in the department of the Seine-Maritime, formerly the Seine-Inférieure. However, I believe the region they migrated to is the Vexin Normand, in the department of the Eure. This is discussed further in note 1 to Chapter Two.

8. The census of 1906 for Avesnes-les-Aubert (Archives départementales du Nord, M 474/38) lists the family of Pierre Gardez with four daughters at home: Edvige [sic], Anatolie, Espérance, and Marie. Elsewhere in the town lived Lucie (mother of Alfred), who was married to Alfred Guidez; Palmyre, married to Paul Noirman (apparently Mémé confused the two brothers-in-law); and Léandre, her brother.

Chapter Two

1. There was no town or village by the name of Avay in the department of the Seine-Inférieure at the period. The kind of large commercial farm specializing in wheat and sugar beets that Mémé describes is rare in Normandy. The only region where it is common is in the Vexin Normand, which lies between Rouen and Paris. The Vexin Normand was (and is) in the department of the Eure.

Writing about the Vexin, Jules Sion remarked in 1909: "This region of plains with flat, monotonous horizons is unique because of its colossal farms. . . . In no other part of eastern Normandy does one see such large farm buildings; grouped around a square courtyard are barns and stables, all kept meticulously clean, vast buildings which recall not a local style but the etchings from a treatise on agricultural architecture. . . . Their origin is probably linked to English agronomers' experiments or those of the Beauce [a large-scale wheat-growing region to the west of Paris]" (Sion, *Les paysans de la Normandie orientale* [Paris, 1909], p. 414). One of the towns of the Vexin is Etrépagny (population about 2,400 in 1906). In the period of Mémé's memories, I discovered, Etrépagny had a large sugar refinery and a hamlet called Saint-Martin (see Louis Passy, "Des mouvements de la population dans le département de l'Eure et le retour à la terre," in Passy, *Mélanges scientifiques et littéraires* [Paris, 1907], pp. 313–56). There is no place called Avay in the Vexin.

It is highly unlikely that the Gardez family went to Dieppe, which is miles away from the large-scale farms of the Vexin, on their migration. The local railroad stop for Etrépagny would be Andelys; the nearby large city, Rouen, which *is* in the Seine-Inférieure.

2. The teams of reapers from Flanders were part of another seasonal migration that followed the grain harvest.

Chapter Three

1. The age Mémé gives for her mother at various dates is consistent with her age on the 1906 census, in which her birth date is given as 1848. However, the same birth date is given in the census listing for her father. The Gardez parents' ages are also given as identical in Mémé's birth and marriage registrations. The evidence suggests, then, that her parents were the same age. According to the 1906 census, her nephew Alfred was born in 1905, not 1906.

2. The 1906 census lists the Santer (a variant spelling) family, with Auguste, the eldest child, born 1888 (consistent with the marriage registration of Mémé and Auguste in 1909), but with ten younger children in the household. The youngest Santer was born in 1906. I am certain this is the correct Santer family, because not only is the son's birth date correct, but the parents' names are the same as in the marriage registration.

Chapter Four

1. The marriage date is correct. The witnesses were her sister Lucie and her husband, Alfred Guidez, and her sister Edvige [sic]. There is quite a contrast in the signatures of the participants in the marriage register. Mémé's handwriting is neat and schooled; the others signed in wavering, crudely formed script. Auguste wrote his "Santer" in a barely legible hand.

2. Actually, the Santerres were not as old as Mémé's parents. Their birth dates were 1862 and 1863. They were poorer not because of their age but because they had several dependent children still at home and unable to work.

Chapter Five

1. See Chapter Two, note 1. The closest city was probably Andelys.

Chapter Six

1. Bastille Day, the French national holiday.

2. Mitry is to the east of Paris. The Brie region, to the east and south of Paris, is another large-scale agricultural area, specializing in grain and sugar beets. There is still a large sugar refinery in Mitry.

Chapter Seven

1. Mémé probably means that the driver used the familiar *tu*, rather than the more formal *vous*, for "you." The *tu* form was reserved in most of France for close kin, very old friends, or distinct inferiors.

Chapter Eight

1. Mémé errs here: women did not have the vote in France in 1936. (They received the suffrage in 1945, at the end of World War II.) Mémé is telling her husband's life story here, as at other points when she discusses the public arena, rather than the private. Al-

though she comments on her thoughts and feelings about these events, she took no direct part in them.

Chapter Nine

1. Apparently the refinery was run by the Todt Organization, a German unit that took over factory and agricultural production in occupied Europe for German military and civilian consumption.